THE
EMIGRATION
DIALECTIC

THE EMIGRATION DIALECTIC

Puerto Rico and the USA

by Manuel Maldonado-Denis

International Publishers, New York

Library of Congress Cataloging in Publication Data

Maldonado-Denis, Manuel, 1933-
    The emigration dialectic.

    Translation of Puerto Rico y Estados Unidos.
    Bibliography: p.
    1. Puerto Ricans in the United States—
Social conditions.   I. Title.
E184.P85M3413   304.8'73'07295   80-16640
ISBN 0-7178-0596-4
ISBN 0-7178-0563-8 (pbk.)

To:
Manuel Emiliano, my *compañero*
of the present and the future

TRANSLATOR'S NOTE

Gunnar Myrdal once said that criticism of the theory of underdevelopment leads inevitably to criticism of the system itself, and that there is no room for "diplomacy" in social research. Professor Manuel Maldonado-Denis has dealt a serious blow to those who have attempted to see Puerto Rican emigration within the "neutral" and "diplomatic" arena of bourgeois social science. I am proud to have been asked to translate this analysis.

I want to thank Louise Gross, *compañera* and secretary of the Oakes College Steno Pool of the University of California at Santa Cruz, who, because she believed in this book, went beyond the call of duty in preparing the final typed draft. I would also like to thank Steve Cochran, *compañero,* student and compatriot, who helped with the bibliography and tracked down the English sources used in the original Spanish edition. Thanks also to the University of California at Santa Cruz, whose research grant made possible my conferring with Professor Maldonado-Denis in Puerto Rico.

ROBERTO SIMÓN CRESPI

CONTENTS

LIST OF TABLES

I have lived in the monster and I know his
entrails and my weapon is David's sling.

JOSÉ MARTÍ

PREFACE

Every book—and by this I mean any book—is the product of those sociohistoric conditions in which the book is conceived and nurtured. This book is not nor could it be the exception to this rule. The root which nourishes it has drawn from the many and diverse experiences and communicated to the author from the most diverse levels of scientific and philosophical abstraction. Thus, for example, from the Puerto Rican youth born in the United States to the most sophisticated statistical studies of the subject of emigration: all have left their imprint on this work. The author wishes, of course, to acknowledge his intellectual debt to those who for many years have dedicated themselves to the problems raised by this essay. The distinguished scholarly work done throughout the years by Dr. José Luis Vázquez Calzada deserves special recognition in this case. Nor can we overlook the important contributions of Drs. Eduardo Seda Bonilla, Luis Nieves Falcón and Frank Bonilla, nor those of Professors Juan Angel Silén, José Hernández Alvarez and Adalberto López.

The author is particularly grateful for the generous reception he was given by the Department of Political Science at Queens College of the City University of New York during the academic year 1972-1973, and especially grateful to the President of Queens College, Dr. Joseph P. Murphy; the Chairman of the Department of Political Science, Dr. Henry W. Morton; the Director of the Program of Puerto Rican Studies, Professor Rafael Rodríguez; and the Dean of Students, Dr. Robert Picciotto. In addition, we would like to express here our profound gratitude to Professor Carmen Puigdollers and Professors Antonio Valcárcel-Cervera and Rafael Citrón-Ortiz for all that their support and encouragement have meant to the completion of this book. As for my Puerto Rican students at Queens College, I can only say that if there was some one force which above all others has stimulated my writing this book, they were that force.

The author also wishes to express his gratitude to *compañera* Ivette Torres de Cabrer for her generous assistance in translating into Spanish many of the quotes and references that appear in the book. Here in Puerto Rico, the constant stimulation and the devoted interest of my students in my course on Puerto Rican Emigration have contributed significantly to the correction and polishing of some early problems of focus. The Committee of University Professors of the Puerto Rican Socialist Party (Partido Socialista Puertorriqueño) has also contributed, with that extraordinary encouragement and stimulation it always extends to those engaged in critical thought. Furthermore, there was always the support, either latent or openly extended, of a good number of my colleagues in the Department of Political Science of the University of Puerto Rico.

I would like to express my gratitude for the generous assistance offered to me at every moment by that extraordinary Puerto Rican family, headed by the architect Simón Fracinetti Ruiz. Likewise, I can do no less than profoundly thank Doña Ana Salamanca y Suárez, distinguished secretary, mother and teacher of the Department of Political Science of the University of Puerto Rico.

Since the Spanish publication of *Puerto Rico: A Socio-Historic Interpretation,* our home has been the scene of some natural phenomena: from the domestic cyclone, Carmen Sara; to the tropical hurricane, Alma Patricia; up to that latest addition to tropical phenomenology, an earthquake-power whose name is Manuel Emiliano. To Manuel Emiliano, I dedicate this book, although, as all my other books, it is dedicated also to the great mother earth who has made the garden of our home so fruitful, my *compañera* Alma.

PROLOGUE TO THE ENGLISH LANGUAGE EDITION*

Four years have elapsed since this work first appeared in Spanish. During that time, Puerto Rican political events have taken place with dizzying speed. The deepening structural crisis that United States monopoly capital is now suffering has had such a profound and powerful impact on Puerto Rican social formation that our people appear to be sinking more and more into abject dependency. It is sufficient to read the annual reports submitted by the Planning Board to the Colonial Governor of Puerto Rico during the last four years to verify this fact. In addition, President Carter requested an inter-agency study of Puerto Rico's economic situation from his Secretary of Commerce, Dr. Juanita Kreps. What is known of this report up until now indicates that the Puerto Rican economy is in a state of extreme prostration and that Puerto Rico only survives thanks to the massive transfusions of funds from the United States Federal Government. The immediate effect of these transfusions has been to foster and at the same time reinforce the attitudes of dependency and submission, that have served as the principal bases for the process of hegemonization which U.S. troops imposed in Puerto Rico from the very moment of their arrival on the island in 1898. This phenomenon has profound psychological roots and is not likely to disappear since it goes hand in hand with the creation of a material base for the plan to annex Puerto Rico to the United States as another state of the North American union. If we are to adhere faithfully to the postulates of historical materialism, we cannot avoid a fact of profound historical-social significance: almost fifty percent of the Puerto Rican labor force finds itself outside of the productive process. In order, therefore, to place the Puerto Rican economy on its feet again, we would need the powers denied us by our

*This book was published almost simultaneously by Siglo XXI in Mexico, with the title *Puerto Rico y Estados Unidos: Emigracion y Colonialismo* (1976) and by Casa de las Americas in Cuba with the title *En las entranas: un analisis sociohistorico de la emigración puertorriqueña* (winner of the Casa de las Americas Essay Award, 1976).

present colonial condition. Even more, once national independence has been obtained, the reconstruction of a battered economy and society would be a gigantic challenge to our people as a result of the devastation brought about by a dependent capitalism cemented over the colonialism we have suffered for eight decades.

The situation of the Puerto Rican community in the United States offers an equally desolate picture. With the capitalist depression, the condition of Puerto Ricans has grown worse during the last four years. We can observe that the phenomenon which Marx called pauperism, and which today some sociologists have persisted in calling "marginality," is illustrated with singular severity among Puerto Ricans who reside in the metropolis. This has brought about a considerable increase in the number of Puerto Ricans who have chosen to return to the national territory during the last five years. (See final chapter.) It is in this sense that we have emphasized the pertinence of the concepts of relative overpopulation and of an industrial reserve army which we have used in the first chapter of this book. It becomes obvious that the economic growth of Puerto Rico during the 1945-1960 period was directly related to the extraordinary and rapid process of capital accumulation in which the United States, as the hegemonic capitalist power, played the leading role after World War II. Once that process of capital accumulation either stagnates or runs its course, we observe the repulsion—and not the attraction—of the emigrants' labor force, a process which is the inverse of the process of the absorption of the large contingents of labor that was experienced during the period just pointed out. This is a reality that can be felt, not only in the United States, but in all of Western Europe. Yet it has been revealed with singular intensity in the area of the Caribbean since, as we know, it is an exporting region not only of raw materials but also of a cheap and abundant labor force to the countries of the capitalist center.

When I look at the book now, in retrospect, it seems to me that this problem did not receive the attention it deserved in its first edition. I now understand that it required a more profound analysis of the productive factor—i.e., the labor force—as well as of the implications of this study for a better understanding of the mechanisms of exploitation used by monopoly capital not only in Puerto Rico but in the entire Caribbean area. In any case, the exploitation suffered by Puerto Rico as a colony of the United States can in no way be completely explained by the abundant profits that the large transnational companies reap from their investments in Puerto Rico (estimated at more than twelve billion dollars), profits directly connected to the economic program that exempts them from paying taxes on the island. In order to understand perfectly the exploitation suffered by our people, it would be necessary to record and itemize everything that the uninterrupted supply of a labor force, the cost of whose production and reproduction falls wholly on Puerto Rican society, means for U.S. capital. I am clarifying this because the ideologues of colonialism and capitalism attempt to distort the significance of this labor supply in order to present us with a vision of the United States investing more in Puerto Rico than it takes from the island in profits. We do not pretend to avoid the question regarding the transfer payments carried out by the United States government in Puerto Rico, especially those payments that imply the massive transfer of funds (800 million dollars) for the food stamps program (for which more than sixty percent of Puerto Rican families qualify). Therefore, the importance of this Caribbean colony can only be fully understood if one takes into account the strategic interests of the United States in Puerto Rico, especially the major significance that the most important North American naval installation in the entire North Atlantic—the Roosevelt Roads naval base in Ceiba—has within the imperialist designs. The U.S. empire does not pay one penny to the Puerto Rican people for this enormous facility, the supply center for the Polaris submarines and cornerstone of the naval complex made up by Ceiba and the adjacent islands of Vieques and Culebra. We can say as much about the exploitation suffered by Puerto Ricans who have emigrated and are still emigrating to the United States. We repeat what we have said on many occasions: Puerto Ricans constitute the lowest rung of the social ladder of U.S. society. This condition accompanies the racial discrimination that permeates and corrodes that society and condemns all the so-called "minorities" within it to a precarious condition in the heart of the North American social structure. Puerto Ricans share, therefore, a common destiny of racial and social discrimination with Native Americans, Chicanos, Afro-Americans, Asian-Americans, in short, with all those ethnic groups that fall under the category of "non-whites" in the United States.

Upon reviewing the ideas on the subject of Puerto Rican emigration that I have discussed earlier, I have discovered that the ideology of neo-Malthusianism still prevails as dogma in our society. According to what we have been able to observe, Malthus' ghost refuses to die in the

Puerto Rico of today. In spite of the recent discoveries that fix the mineral wealth of the island in several billions of dollars, and in spite of the evidence that tends to show that there is an eighty percent probability that there are oil deposits on the northeastern coast of Puerto Rico, the official ideology—supported by both colonialist political parties—maintains that we are a small, poor and overpopulated island and that our only alternative for survival is through mass birth control, exportation of our labor force and acceptance of massive infusions of U.S. dollars. We have already observed (Chapter 2) how this ideology, put into practice, led to the sterilization of one-third of all Puerto Rican women of child-rearing age. If it is indeed certain that the political party that presently holds power in the colony—the Partido Nuevo Progresista (with annexionist tendencies)—has discontinued programs of mass sterilization of women which reached its zenith under the administration of the Partido Popular Democratico (1972–76), nevertheless the neo-Malthusian ideological suppositions continue to influence. Since the Partido Nuevo Progresista wants to prepare Puerto Rico for the transition towards annexation to the United States as a state of that nation, its principal emphasis is in the progressive increment of funds from the metropolis. Seen from the annexionist perspective, Puerto Rico is an integral part of the United States and is presently in transit toward a political condition that will definitively and permanently cement the annexation of the Puerto Rican people to the political power of the metropolis. According to that annexionist vision, what is taking place in the demographic flow between Puerto Rico and the United States is, plainly and simply, an internal migration among citizens of one and the same nation, but not an emigration from one nation to another. That is why we are again emphasizing that the term emigration is the most correct to describe the involuntary exile of Puerto Ricans in the United States. One must insist on the fact that Puerto Rico is a Latin American nation that has been annexed by force by the North American empire, or, in other words, that our island belongs to the United States as war booty from the Spanish-American War. Finally, it is necessary to clarify that the so-called imbalance between resources and population in Puerto Rico is not the exclusive product, as has been claimed, of excessive population growth. There is no doubt that population growth is a factor of great importance in economic growth (or lack of growth). But we must emphasize the even more significant fact, that underdevelopment and poverty obey the mechanisms of exploitation which capitalism in its imperialist monopolistic stage has maintained for more than two-thirds of the world population.

There are some additional matters that I would like to touch on, although very briefly, in this prologue.

In the first place, it is important to emphasize the fact that a more thorough study of Puerto Rican emigration before World War II is necessary. The Center of Puerto Rican Studies of the City University of New York (CUNY) has carried out important efforts in that direction.[1] The publication of the excellent book that collects the memoirs of the great Puerto Rican fighter, Bernardo Vega, unquestionably contributes to the clarification of the character of the Puerto Rican and Hispanic resident in the metropolis during the period between the two world wars. There is no doubt that this renewed interest in the study of the Puerto Rican emigration experience—a problem about which we can not remain indifferent—will deepen our understanding of that experience.

In the second place, I would like to emphasize the importance for the Puerto Rican political process of the return to the island of some 150,000 Puerto Ricans during the last five years. Preliminary studies, like that of Professor Saul Ponce de León at the request of the Centro de Investigaciones Sociales of the University of Puerto Rico, tend to show that a majority of those who return lean towards the political alternative of annexation. We said (Chapter 7) that these compatriots, in addition, had difficulty adjusting to the new Puerto Rican environment. We likewise tied this phenomenon to the problem of cultural assimilation of Puerto Ricans to the ruling world view in the metropolis. In any case, the problem of the so-called "Neoricans" is a very real one, which demands a thorough analysis that maintains an empathy and sympathy toward those Puerto Ricans who have been stripped of their language, their history and their culture and who seek their own forms of cultural expression. This ought to be perfectly understood, not as a simple intellectual expression, but as a guide for political action.

In the third place, we consider that the problems relevant to the cultural assimilation of Puerto Ricans (in the colony as well as in the metropolis) can not be resolved by means of political decrees that emanate from a particular ideology, but rather must be studied with a critical spirit that is attentive to Gramsci's maxim that the truth is always revolutionary. We have stated (Chapter 6) that the difference between the cultural assimilation of Puerto Ricans in Puerto Rico and in the United States is one of degree and not of kind, or, in other words, that it is a question of the relative intensity of a very profound problem that takes place in both poles of the colony-metropolis relation. We reaffirm that judgment. We believe it necessary to make the distinction that the adhesion to a national culture is a sociological fact of great collective significance which requires as a prior condition the knowledge and recognition, on the part of the individual who adheres to this culture, of the historical and social roots that have contributed to shape that nationality. This presupposes a linking with some historical and political processes that will permit the Puerto Rican to identify himself—that is, to find his identity—within the multiplicity of alternative visions that imperialism itself creates and procreates in its attempts at ideological obfuscation. To identify oneself with Puerto Rico is to identify with its great national and social struggles, to recognize that those struggles take place within a national context, and to recognize that they even take place outside of the national territory so long as one-third of our nation lives outside of this territory. Furthermore, the struggle of Puerto Ricans in Puerto Rico and in the metropolis is part of a much broader and more comprehensive one: the struggle against imperialism and its designs of oppression on all the peoples of the world. This is a struggle, therefore, which will have the national territory as its principal setting, but which will also be waged wherever the unbreakable will of Puerto Ricans against discrimination and prejudice is affirmed, whether it be in South Bronx, in el Barrio (East Harlem) or in the agricultural fields of New England.

Lenin informed us, in memorable pages, that every culture contains a profound class dimension. Marx himself had told us that the ideas of the ruling class were the ruling ideas of every epoch. Both thinkers also indicate to us that subordinate classes seek their own forms of cultural expression as opposed to those of the ruling culture. So also, colonial peoples develop their own forms of expression, their own ways of demonstrating their resistance to the colonizing power. Puerto Rico and those Puerto Ricans who want to continue being Puerto Rican, even in the face of the most merciless imperialist cultural penetration, are an irrefutable proof that our people have not given up their will to struggle. The Puerto Rican working class is the numerically superior class in Puerto Rico as well as in the Puerto Rican community residing in the metropolis. To that class will correspond the task of becoming a national and, consequently, hegemonic class in order to serve as the medullary force of the Puerto Rican liberation struggle. Needless to say, in that process the portion of the Puerto Rican working class that lives in the metropolis will have a principal role to play in the very heart of U.S. capitalist society.

One last reflection. Much is said today about exiles and refugees. As I write these lines, imperialism has unleashed its entire advertising apparatus to misinform world public opinion about the problems generated as a result of the genocidal wars waged against the peoples of Kampuchea and Vietnam by the United States itself. However, those same agencies do not call humanity's attention to the ordeal of the Palestinian people, stripped of their territory and in turn victim of the most bloody oppression by Zionism and imperialism. Nor have they bothered adequately to inform the public about the painful emigratory processes that go hand in hand with the oscillations of capitalism and that imply the uprooting and forced exile of millions of people pushed outside of their respective national territories because of urgent economic needs. One must understand the phenomenon in all its extension and profundity: emigration is one of the modalities of exile. The emigrant is an involuntary exile who abandons his homeland because peripheral and dependent capitalism converts great contingents of workers into objects of exportation toward the highly industrialized capitalist countries. When these countries experience a profound economic crisis—as in the present situation of the capitalist world—they then opt for the processes of repatriation of the labor force which formerly served them as the basis for a rapid process of capitalist accumulation.

The Puerto Ricans who, pushed by economic necessity, have suffered and continue to suffer painful exile in the United States, have never lost the hope of returning to the national territory in order to put an end to their condition as exiles. But for the immense majority of the Puerto Rican community, returning to the homeland is most often unrealistic. Within forced exile, Puerto Rican workers form part of a multi-ethnic working class which suffers capitalist exploitation in its most obvious form. When seen from an internationalist perspective, the fate of the Puerto Rican working class—in Puerto Rico as well as in the United States—is bound to that of the workers of the whole world. That working class has a common enemy everywhere in the world. Faced with that common enemy, the struggle of all peoples for their independence and national liberation is an unavoidable duty of the working class and the parties that represent them. Therefore, in emigration or in exile, in the national territory or in the imperialist metropolis, the desideratum of the Puerto Rican working class will have to be, in the short and long run, that of culminating the liberation struggle of Puerto Rico with the only political solution that would fulfill the interests of that social class: the independence of Puerto Rico.

There is no royal road to science, and only those who do not dread the fatiguing climb of its steep paths have a chance of gaining its luminous summits.

KARL MARX

INTRODUCTION

In the prologue to the sixth Spanish edition of my book, *Puerto Rico: A Socio-Historic Interpretation,* I said, speaking of Puerto Rican emigration:

There has not been, perhaps, a more transcendent event for the destiny of the Puerto Rican nation than the massive exodus of more than a half million Puerto Ricans during the historical period immediately following the end of World War II. We can say, with no fear of being mistaken, that the social process begun in 1945 appears to be an irreversible one, and that the social history of Puerto Rico has to be reexamined in light of this emigration phenomenon and its consequences.

The author first attempted a confrontation with the subject of emigration by means of an epilogue written expressly for the English translation of the book just cited.[1] The epilogue left much to be desired with respect to the profundity and extent of its analysis. This is why I have taken up this task of offering the reader a socio-historic interpretation of Puerto Rican emigration to the United States. From this perspective, the present volume should be seen as a kind of continuation, a necessary sequel, to *Puerto Rico: A Socio-Historical Interpretation.** I would like, however, to make some pertinent and necessary observations before proceeding with the content of the book.

In the first place, the author of this book has not lived—except for one year (1972-1973), when he served as Visiting Professor of Political Science at Queens College of the City University of New York—

Puerto Rico: una interpretación socio-histórica, published originally in Spanish by Mexico's Siglo XXI Editores, appeared in 1969. Six editions of this volume have been published, and on two occasions corrected and expanded (the 4th edition in 1971 and the 6th edition in 1974).

in a direct and palpable way the vital experiences of those who have suffered first-hand the rigors and vicissitudes of Puerto Rican emigration to the United States. This is without doubt an important limitation, since I am unable to give testimony through personal experience of what it really means to live in the subhuman and alienating conditions which make up the daily bread for the immense majority of our compatriots residing in the metropolis. A great part of the works produced in the United States by Puerto Rican authors born and raised there—written, as to be expected, in the English language—consist precisely of the anguished and dreadful expression of what it means to be Puerto Rican within the borders of that North American country. So, for example, the poet Pedro Pietri,[2] the writer Piri Thomas,[3] and the psychologist Samuel Betances[4]—from diverse ethical, aesthetic and sociological perspectives—focus on the problems they have experienced in the here and now of their existence as Puerto Ricans.

The weakness that afflicts the greater part of these works, as invaluable as they are as testimonies of a lived reality, lies in the fact that they do not take note of the wider context of a socio-historic interpretation of the Puerto Rican experience, seen, not from the limited optics of the New York ghetto, but rather from the wider perspective of the dialectics between the colony and the metropolis. In other words, we miss in these works that extraordinary ability shown by a George Jackson, capable of connecting his own personal experience in the prison at San Quentin to that entire system of oppression, and which was archetypically illustrated in the society which condemned him to death. A Puerto Rican George Jackson, endowed with the theoretical and practical ability to interpret the Puerto Rican reality in the United States, not merely on the level of testimony or protest but also through that flight of theory that Marx considered indispensable to every efficient revolutionary action, would make the interpretation that I intend to outline in this work perhaps superfluous. Meanwhile, I have ventured to dedicate myself to a project before whose magnitude I can do no less than proceed "with fear and trembling."

In the second place, a great part of the bibliography on the subject—rather extensive to be sure, if we are to judge by the bibliography offered us a few years ago by Dr. Clarence Senior—is in English and is essentially the product of U.S. sociologists, demographers or historians.[5] Needless to say, this fact in itself does not disqualify a sociological work. In fact, the great U.S. sociologist C. Wright Mills offered us one of the most valuable and original interpretations of the Puerto Rican emigration question in a study carried out with a group of collaborators and published in 1950 under the title *The Puerto Rican Journey: New York's Newest Migrants.*[6] What I mean by this observation about this bibliography is that most of the works published by U.S. authors, when they do not fall into the paternalistic trap which seems to ensnare almost all U.S. liberals, have a clear apologetic purpose. In other words, when submitted to the prism of critical thought, works dressed up in all the paraphernalia of scientific analysis end up being mere ideological excursions directed toward the rationalization of the actual situation. (From this point of view, if anyone deserves the title of "Principal Ideologue" of Puerto Rican emigration to the United States, it is Dr. Clarence Senior himself, whose most recent works denote an invariable ability to see light in the middle of darkness.) Consequently, the production of critical works on the problem of Puerto Rican emigration is relatively lean, even if we do not overlook the contributions of sociologists and historians such as José Luis Vázquez Calzada, Luis Nieves Falcón, Eduardo Seda Bonilla, Juan Angel Silén and Frank Bonilla.

We consider it essential to point out that we are still lacking a work of global character which can capture that "organic" totality (Marx) which constitutes the phenomenon of Puerto Rican emigration to the United States. In order to accomplish this goal, it is necessary that emigration be seen as an integral part of a more extensive whole: Puerto Rican society. For this reason, we should see Puerto Rican society on the one hand in relation to the North American metropolis, and on the other, in relation to U.S. society in so much as it gathers in its womb Puerto Ricans who emigrate from Puerto Rico. What is required is a method of "consecutive approximations" to a socio-historic phenomenon, whose dialectically interrelated roots have to be sought as much here in Puerto Rico as among the resident Puerto Rican community in the United States. The question should be seen, in turn, in the wider context of the emigration movements which are a product of the very nature of the capitalist system on a world level. In this sense, the ordeal of the Puerto Ricans who live in the New York ghettos or who work as *braceros* (agricultural day laborers) in the fields of New England is not an ordeal unknown to the Algerian who sweeps the streets in Paris or Marseilles, nor to the Afro-Antillian from the West Indies who lives in London or Manchester. In the same way, that exploitation is not unknown to Afro-Americans, Chicanos, Native North American Indians, Asian-Americans, nor to any other resident ethnic group in the metropolis, already especially those who are classified as "non-whites" with U.S. society.

This work, therefore, has some goals which are very modest, but at the same time ambitious. They are modest because we are setting out from the limitation inevitable to any study written by a Puerto Rican who lives on the island of Puerto Rico. They are ambitious, because we intend to interpret a reality from a critical perspective which has in turn two focuses: the Puerto Ricans in the colony and the Puerto Ricans in the metropolis. The reader is asked to understand this work deals with a task of enormous span, especially when we approach it with the limitations of space and extension imposed by an essay which is socio-historic in character.

It will be observed that we are using the term Puerto Rican "emigration" instead of the term Puerto Rican "migration." We are dealing, of course, with something more than a mere semantic question. As we have maintained on repeated occasions, Puerto Rico is a Latin American nation which has been under U.S. colonization since 1898. In spite of the fact that we Puerto Ricans were declared United States citizens in 1917 (over and above the opposition of the Puerto Rican leaders at that time), to accept that the exodus to the United States is a simple "internal migration" would be equivalent to accepting the claim that Puerto Rico is now an integral and indissoluble part of the United States. The concept of "migration" has been used as an ideological weapon by the defenders of the colonialism under which we Puerto Ricans suffer. We do not deny the validity of the concept of migration when describing phenomena such as the movement of great multitudes of people from the rural areas to the cities, but we cannot accept its validity when it refers to the mass movements of our compatriots to the metropolis. That is why we are using the term Puerto Rican emigration in this book.

Some final remarks. Let us proceed first from what this book is not nor intends to be:

In the first place, *we do not purport to offer here a polished statistical survey of Puerto Rican emigration.* We do not mean in any way to slight statistics. On the contrary, the reader will note that we refer to them throughout this work. But we are on guard against the traps of empiricism and positivism, and we do not want to convert this study into a simple exercise in the accumulation of figures. Anyone interested in the most important and basic figures *which should be known* with respect to Puerto Rican emigration, can find them in the statistical appendix attached to this book.

In the second place, this book *is not a study in demography,* nor will it be limited to viewing the problem of population as a biological phenomenon. The reader will not find this book limited to the perspective of one discipline only but rather an interdisciplinary approach which can help us in the clarification of the subject.

In the third place, the author of this book does not have—nor could he have—the solution to the problems of Puerto Ricans in the United States. The true solution to those problems will be, needless to say, the product of the unity between practice and theory which takes place day after day and will come about as a result of the daily action of our people who have emigrated. There are no magical formulas nor panaceas, but rather the concrete reality of revolutionary popular action.

The objectives of this essay are modest but not therefore less comprehensive: in the first place, this essay proposes to analyze and integrate the entire complex network of social relations that define the Puerto Rican experience in the United States. Relations of this nature cannot be seen in abstraction from the Puerto Rican reality in certain determined historical moments. That is why we are focussing on the Puerto Rican reality from a socio-historic perspective, equally in Puerto Rico as well as among Puerto Ricans who have emigrated to the metropolis.

In the second place, this work intends to examine the problem of Puerto Rican emigration by proceeding from a theoretical outline capable of rationally explaining the socio-historic causes and effects of this social phenomenon. The theory that has served us as guide has been historical materialism. We believe that this theory serves to explain scientifically the emigration phenomenon, while at the same time offering the models of historical action for overcoming this phenomenon.

Lastly, this essay is a conscious negation of the spurious principle of "ethical neutrality" in the social sciences. Very much to the contrary, we are dealing here with a work committed to the struggle of Puerto Ricans—those of the Island and those who reside in the metropolis— who fight to break with all those structures and practices that maintain us in the condition of a people exploited by imperialism. We will try to be objective but in no way will we be impartial. Our place will always be there: alongside the Puerto Rican working people who fight for independence, national liberation and socialism.

*In the social production of their existence,
men inevitably enter into definite relations,
which are independent of their will, namely
relations of production appropriate to a
given stage in the development of their
material forces of production.*

KARL MARX

1

MODE OF PRODUCTION
AND EMIGRATION

In the entire body of Marxist theory, there is perhaps no concept more
fertile or more suggestive than that of "mode of production." This
concept, together with that of "economic-social formation," has contributed decisively towards guiding Marxism along the road of critical
thought, away from scholastic rigidity on the one hand and from
rhetorical clichés on the other.[1] One can observe everywhere today—
and with extraordinary impact in Latin America—a rebirth of Marxist
studies, a discipline and seriousness in analysis which honors the best
tradition of Marxist sociology. We would like to substantiate this fact
since, in Puerto Rico, critical thought based on Marxist categories is a
kind of outcast in the entire academic system. The "paradigm" for the
social sciences in Puerto Rico continues to be the one provided by the
positivist and empiricist ideological blueprints characteristic of the
United States academic system.

    This essay proposes to approach the subject of emigration from a
Marxist perspective. Our point of departure is therefore the following
statement by Marx from his "Preface" in *A Contribution to the
Critique of Political Economy* (1857): "In the social production of their
existence, men inevitably enter into definite relations, which are independent of their will, namely relations of production appropriate to a
given stage in development of their material forces of production." We
believe it imperative to stress this point of *the social production of their*

existence, since this is the very center of our focus. This social production is organized in a definite way, and the relations of production—which capitalism fetishizes so as to conceal the social and therefore *human* character of these relations—imply that "mode of production of material life conditions the process of social, political and spiritual life in general." Marx distinguishes between different historical modes of production. His principal analysis, however, is aimed at the capitalist mode of production, which is the dominant mode of production in Puerto Rico. But we find a complication that did not exist in the society that served as the model for Marx's analysis in his time, that is, nineteenth-century England. We are referring to the fact that Puerto Rico is a colonial society which finds itself under the direct sovereignty of the capitalist metropolis of the world. This has, of course, profound consequences for our analysis, since Puerto Rico, under its present system cannot transcend the limits of being a peripheral (Amin), dependent capitalist, and at the same time, a colonial country. From that point of view, we tend to agree with the criterion of Juan Carlos Garavaglia, who, referring to the modes of production and social formations in colonial territories, tells us:

> We think that colonial economic-social formations would not have a hegemonic mode of production in Marx's "classical" sense, because in the last instance the dominion of the system is external to the dominated territories . . . It is evident that if there is something that gives sense to the whole system in our colonial territories, that element is *the colonial relation* and not this or that native mode of production.[2]

Following this same line of reasoning, Ciro F. S. Cardoso speaks of a slave-colonial mode of production while the author of these lines speaks of present-day Puerto Rico as ruled by the capitalist-colonial mode of production.[3]

The question transcends simple semantic quarrels, and deals with problems concerning the most adequate focuses for understanding our complex social reality. We do not have the slightest doubt that the categories of "mode of production" and "economic-social formation" serve to shed light on the problem of the emigration of Puerto Ricans, especially since they allow us to identify the phenomenon as part of a global reality.

Therefore, what will be of interest to us are the different stages in the development of the capitalist-colonial mode of production in Puerto Rico, especially as they speak to and are directly related to the emigration phenomenon. So, the transition from the social formations characteristic of an economy centered in the *haciendas* to those of one based on the large sugar plantation, and likewise the transition from the plantation to the programs of "Fomento Económico" (Economic Development) in its different phases, will serve as the parameters of our analysis.

We will try to show that emigration is not a fortuitous nor accidental social phenomenon, but rather something profoundly connected to the capitalist-colonial mode of production. The focus of this essay will therefore be to understand Puerto Rican emigration as part of a more extensive and more comprehensive reality. That is why we have begun with a reference to the central concept that will guide this study.

There are two ways of focusing on the problems of emigration from a scientific-social perspective. One consists of seeing the problem as an isolated, particular and self-contained social phenomenon. The other perspective requires a global, general focus, where the problem of emigration is seen within the wider perspective of the problems and disorders that affect a society as an organic whole. A study group of Latin Americans of the Comisión de Población y Desarrollo (Commission on Population and Development) of the Consejo Latinoamericano de Ciencias Sociales (CLACSO, the Latin American Council of Social Sciences) tried to place the phenomenon of emigration within a structural context, precisely from that global perspective. The conclusions of this group have been collected in an important study which, under the title *Migración y desarrollo—consideraciones teóricas y aspectos socioeconómicos y políticos* (Migration and Development: Theoretical Considerations and Socio-economic and Political Aspects), was published by CLACSO in 1973. The question that concerns us is placed in its proper perspective by Omar Argüello in a work entitled "Migración y cambio estructural" (Migration and Structural Change) which contrasts the focuses which we are analyzing in this work:

> According to one perspective, this social structure is composed of a set of norms and values which appear as given and not as the product of an historical development; norms and values which would be accepted by the whole of society and transmitted to new generations through the process of socialization. The basic unit upon which these norms and values operate, determining his conduct, is the individual. In this theoretical perspective, the possibilities for the transformation of society are identified as the appearance of changes in the individuals themselves, manifested at a psycho-

logical level by the emergence of new attitudes and the adoption of new norms and values. When these changes reach the majority of the population, we find a new society, through the mechanism of "modernization."

While from the other perspective—which is the one we consider correct from the point of view of the problems and perspectives of emigrations and internal migrations in Puerto Rico—, Argüello tells us:

> We believe that internal migrations should be seen as a social process of population redistribution within the context of a global society, characterized by a definite productive structure, belonging to the kind and degree of development reached within an historical process, which is carried out by different social and political groups which have succeeded in imposing their interests and values on the whole of that society.
>
> Within this historical and structural context, the changes that occur in that population redistribution are results of changes that take place at the level of the productive structure and the structure of domination, remembering of course that determination is never merely unidirectional and therefore these population changes in many cases will produce changes in the productive structure, in the system of domination and in the ideological forms that legitimize it.[4]

In other words, abandoning a sociohistoric focus on migrations would condemn us to the sterility of a strict psychological focus, more properly belonging to sociological schools whose paradigm is the positivist or empiricist focus characteristic of bourgeois social science.[5] It is this last focus which—with rare exception—has predominated among those who study Puerto Rican emigration, especially when dealing with studies carried out by sociologists or demographers from the metropolis.

Let us take note of the structural changes which have taken place in the Puerto Rican economy since 1940, a crucial historical moment in the contemporary history of Puerto Rico. With the slogan of "Bread, Land and Liberty" a political party of clear populist profile, whose pseudo-revolutionary rhetoric will clothe itself with the occult image of reformism, arrives to exercise colonial power in our homeland. It is a populism we should understand, in the description of Professor Octavio Ianni, as "a mass movement that appears in the center of the structural ruptures that accompany the crisis of the world capitalist system and the corresponding crises of Latin American oligarchies."[6] In fact, already by 1940, the economic system of sugar plantations, which will signal the whole systematic process of expropriation which Professor Angel Quintero Rivera[7] has described as one characterized by the passage from an economy centered in the *haciendas* to one centered in the plantations, is already found to be in a stage of chronic stagnancy. We are referring, of course, to the expropriation of Puerto Rican landowners who lose their lands in gigantic strides in the face of the irresistible push of the large United States sugar companies. This process will begin, as we pointed out in another book,[8] with the adoption by the Partido Popular Democrático of the program known as "Fomento Industrial" under the direction of Teodoro Moscoso. What the Partido Popular Democrático proposes, then, is to stimulate the economic growth of Puerto Rico through *industrialization*. The decision does not take into account—nor could it in the case of Puerto Rico—the needs of an exporting national bourgeoisie, whose primary goal was to introduce in Puerto Rico an economic system founded on the *"substitution" of imports*. Rather, it is conceived as an experiment, namely, to serve as a kind of "showcase" for establishing medium-sized and small businesses which, attracted by tax exemptions, cheap and abundant labor and direct access to the U.S. market, wished to be established on our Island. The program of "Fomento Económico" did not propose to establish a basis for a self-sustaining development of the Puerto Rican economy, but rather simply to appease through an economic *growth* predicated on the massive injections of foreign capital, principally United States capital.* What *is* altered in the change from the sugar economy based on the plantation to the new industrialization is merely the *form* of dependency, not its substance. The changes that took place in the postwar capitalist economy with the development of monopoly capital and the resulting displacement of medium and small businesses by the large transnational companies created a favorable setting for a project that can serve as "model" for Latin American countries faced with the problem of anti-development. As on past occasions, Puerto Rico must serve as the Caribbean's experimental center for the domination designs of U.S. imperialism.

When the program of "Fomento Económico" is founded in 1947, the Partido Popular Democrático abandons its populist rhetoric in order to embrace some plans of economic growth which would have a dual orientation: to formulate the solution to the social problems of the

*For a confirmation of the validity of this assertion, see the article by the present Director of the Department of the Budget, Dr. Jaime Santiago Méndez, "Puerto Rico—Presente y Futuro Económico—Hacia una Nueva Estrategia," *Boletín de Gerencia Administrativa,* January–February, 1975.

Island from a technocratic point of view, and to give this technocratic orientation the markings of an economic theory of development. It would be enough just to read the articles and speeches of the principal ideologues of the "Fomento" Administration in that historic moment in order to corroborate this assessment.*

The Puerto Rican economy embarks on a new step, facing, in this process of industrialization, the problem pointed out by Paul Singer:

> The division of labor between advanced countries and those of colonial economies, established in the last century and strengthened in the present one, specified the most recent agreements with respect to the *natural resources* of the countries of colonial economies in function of the needs of the former. This type of international division of labor did not supply the labor force of the countries of colonial economies with any special ability that could provide them with comparative advantages in the world market, independently of their natural resources.[9]

In other words, the profound changes in the economic and social structures, which every process of industrialization produces, tend to dislocate the traditional agricultural economy without providing at the same time the necessary mechanisms to absorb the labor force displaced by the new system. This is in line with the unplanned nature—at the world level—of a capitalist economy.

With the program of "Fomento," Puerto Rican agriculture begins its definitive decline. A recent study helps us to examine closely the magnitude of the change by indicating that the total number of agricultural workers (14 years of age and older) declined from 120,000 in 1952-1953 to 75,000 in 1970-1971.[10] The Report of the Governor's Labor Committee on "Opportunities of employment, education and training," moreover, states that

> in accordance with the projections of the Planning Board, the total employment in agriculture will be reduced from 75,000 to 36,000 between 1972 and 1985, for an average annual drop of 3,000. Most of that reduction, however, will take place by 1985, when employment will tend to stabilize at 36,000.**

In accordance with these statistics, the reader will be able to judge whether Puerto Rican agriculture has been relegated to a purely

*A good taste of this ideology can be found in the special issue of the journal *La Torre* dedicated to Puerto Rican emigration. *La Torre* (Río Piedras), year IV, no. 13, January-March, 1956.
**This report was submitted to the Governor of Puerto Rico in 1973. We will refer to it again later in this study.

secondary place within the economic strategy of the present government.

A study on the problem of internal emigration in Puerto Rico, by Professor Marcia Rivera de Quintero of the Planning Board, contributes to putting things in their proper perspective. This study demonstrates the structural character of the rural-urban exodus, and emphasizes the accelerated process of depopulation in the countryside which threatens to convert many towns in the interior of the Island into ghost-towns. Using validated statistical proof, Professor Rivera de Quintero verifies the way in which drastic changes have taken place in the distribution of the population between countryside and city, concluding with the following observations:

> Puerto Rico follows the rural-urban model of the developed countries of the Western Hemisphere. The development of a different economic structure based on manufacturing instead of agriculture is one of the phenomena which serve to explain this rapid urban expansion. The tendency is clearly towards concentration in urban areas, the tight relationship between the process of industrialization and the process of urbanization here becoming evident. Sixty years ago, 80% of the Puerto Rican population lived in a rural setting. Today, 58.1% live in urban sectors . . .

> The drastic changes in the population of Puerto Rico are a result of external or internal migration rather than a result of the differences in the natural increment of the population . . .

> From 1950 to 1960 and from 1960 to 1970, only the municipalities near San Juan had increments in population.[11]

We quote extensively from this study because it allows us to examine closely the nature and extent of the changes that have taken place in Puerto Rican society from the beginning of the "Fomento" Program. That is to say, we are able to grasp clearly that this dislocation of Puerto Rican agriculture—and the ensuing uprooting of its rural population—is the result of profound changes in the structure of the Puerto Rican economy and not the result of mere individual decisions arrived at because of fortuitous events. Seen in that context, Dr Vázquez Calzada's following claim acquires greater significance: "For the most part, the emigrants come from the rural zones of Puerto Rico. By the last decades, more than 60% of those who moved to the United States came from the rural zone."[12] The facility of communication with the metropolis has greatly reduced the need for the temporary sojourn in San Juan as a point of departure for the continent. As a general rule, today's emigrants pass through San Juan in transit to the metropolis. Therefore, they are coming out of a rural setting to a predominantly urban one, and the majority settle in the large U.S. urban centers. Therefore, the entire process of Puerto Rican emigration to the United States should be seen as the product of economic decisions that are responses to the needs of the world capitalist division of labor, rather than to the concrete needs of those affected, directly and adversely, by the process itself. Whether under the plantation economy, centered on the one-crop production of sugar cane, or under industrialization, based on the attraction of small and medium-sized businesses or gigantic petrochemical enterprises, it is certain that the masses of workers and peasants are those who have suffered the greatest hardships from the process of the exodus to the metropolis. These workers and peasants have not presided over this process, but rather have been its victims. In this sense, they have repeated the historical process of proletarianization, which Marx saw as an integral part of capitalism, especially the process which refers to the creation of a "relative surplus-population," which is a product of the general laws of capitalist accumulation.

It is now practically commonplace that one of the principal instruments of imperialism's counterrevolutionary activities is based on the alleged "population explosion" and its presumed panacea: birth control. This is actually imperialism's attempt to revive the polemic between Marx and Malthus, in agreement, needless to say, with Malthus. This ideology has been adopted and put into practice by the colonial government of Puerto Rico during the last thirty years.

Within the framework of capitalism in its competitive phase, abundant labor constitutes a factor which tends to depress the exchange value of labor and to lower the value, therefore, of the price of human labor on the capitalist market. Marx makes this plain when he wrote that:

> The industrial reserve army, during the periods of stagnation and average prosperity, weighs down the active labor-army; during the periods of over-production and paroxysm, it holds its pretensions in check. Relative surplus-population is therefore the pivot upon which the law of demand and supply of labor works. It confines the field of action of this law within the limits absolutely convenient to the activity of exploitation and to the domination of capital.[13]

Today, when in all of Latin America and in the underdeveloped world in general we see launched, as part of imperialist ideology, the thesis of the harmful effects of the "population explosion" and its consequences, it is important to remember Marx's polemic with Malthus, especially Marx's very keen observation of Malthus:

> The laboring population therefore produces, along with the accumulation of capital produced by it, the means by which itself is made relatively superfluous, is turned into a relative surplus-population; and it does this to an always increasing extent. This is a law of population peculiar to the capitalist mode of production; and in fact every special historic mode of production has its own special laws of population, historically valid within its limits alone. An abstract law of population exists for plants and animals only, and only in so far as man has not interfered with them.

Following this same line of reasoning, Marx affirms in the very next line of *Capital:*

> But if a surplus laboring population is a necessary product of accumulation or of the development of wealth on a capitalist basis, this surplus-population becomes, conversely, the lever of capitalistic accumulation, nay, a condition of existence of the capitalist mode of production. It forms a disposable industrial reserve army, that belongs to capital quite as absolutely as if the latter had bred it at its own cost.[14]

In our judgment, the concepts of "relative surplus-population" and "industrial reserve army" help explain not only the very dynamics of the dependent colonial-capitalist regime that prevails in Puerto Rico, but also that they are useful to explain the sociohistoric reasons for the emigratory exodus which at the present moment keeps one-third of our population outside the borders of our national territory. These concepts are also useful for an analysis of the situation of Puerto Ricans in the United States, since they allow for the perception of the problem from a macro-historic perspective that places our people within the wider context of emigration as a global phenomenon resulting from the needs of the capitalist mode of production itself. In this way, the extraction of surplus value can be seen in the light of each concrete situation in which the peculiar form of exploitation is manifested—let's say, on a farm with agricultural workers in the United States or in a petrochemical plant in Puerto Rico. In this way, what is specific and particular in a given sociohistoric situation as well as what is general and universal can be grasped with greater lucidity. Therefore, through the Marxist concepts mentioned, micro-history and macro-history, the national and the international are interconnected. Needless to say, this method of "successive approximations" to the social phenomena which concern us is heuristic, and is not intended to be erected as a dogmatic (and therefore anti-Marxist) master plan. We are concerned with providing a theoretical and methodological apparatus based on Marx's propositions that allow us to understand and to link social reality in a way that is compatible with the best tradition of critical thought.

It is necessary to stress the fact that under the present economic system, there are great masses of workers displaced as much by the structural changes operant in Puerto Rican economy, beginning with the "Fomento," as by the technological transformations that have taken place hand in hand with these changes. The result of this has been the creation of a vast subproletariat composed of people who have been unemployed, underemployed and displaced in general by the very nature of the capitalist system. Once again, Marx's concept of "relative surplus-population" helps us understand better what we are proposing. It is worthwhile to stop and spend some time with this concept since it sheds light on our economic situation. For Marx, relative surplus-population takes on three constant forms.

The floating form:

> In the centres of modern industry—factories, manufactures, ironworks, mines, etc.—the laborers are sometimes repelled, sometimes attracted again in greater masses, the number of those employed increasing on the whole, although in a constantly decreasing proportion to the scale of production. Here the surplus-population exists in the floating form.[15]

The latent form:

> As soon as capitalist production takes possession of agriculture, and in proportion to the extent to which it does so, the demand for an agricultural laboring population falls absolutely, while the accumulation of the capital employed in agriculture advances, without this repulsion being, as in non-agricultural industries, compensated by a greater attraction. Part of the agricultural population is therefore constantly on the point of passing over into an urban or manufacturing proletariat, and on the look-out for circumstances favorable to this transformation. (Manufacture is used here in the sense of all non-agricultural industries.) This source of relative surplus-population is thus constantly flowing. But the constant flow toward the towns presupposes, in the country itself, a constant latent surplus-population, the extent of which becomes evident only when its channels of outlet open to exceptional width. The agricultural laborer is therefore reduced to the minimum of wages, and always stands with one foot already in the swamp of pauperism.[16]

The stagnant form:

> The third category of the relative surplus-population, the stagnant, forms a

part of the active labor army, but with extremely irregular employment. Hence it furnishes to capital an inexhaustible reservoir of disposable labor-power. Its conditions of life sink below the average normal level of the working class; this makes it at once the broad basis of special branches of capitalist exploitation. It is characterised by maximum of working-time, and minimum of wages. We have learnt to know its chief form under the rubric of "domestic industry." It recruits itself constantly from the super-numerary forces of modern industry and agriculture, and specially from those decaying branches of industry where handicraft is yielding to man-ufacture, manufacture to machinery. Its extent grows, as with the extent and energy of accumulation, the creation of a surplus-population advances.[17]

These three categories that refer to the relative surplus-population can be of great use as instruments to analyze a society like ours, with an unemployment of 30 percent of the labor force; and in some towns of the interior this figure reaches more than 50 percent. The transforma-tions suffered by Puerto Rican society, once it had embarked on the road of capitalist industrialization, fit within that theoretical frame-work, in each particular case making clear the applicability of the Marxist analysis.

There is a final category of this Marxist analysis that is of particular importance to us. We are referring to what Marx calls "pauperism." Marx describes this phenomenon in the following way:

The lowest sediment of the relative surplus-population finally dwells in the sphere of pauperism. Exclusive of vagabonds, criminals, prostitutes, in a word, the "dangerous" classes, this layer of society consists of three catego-ries. First, those able to work. One need only glance superficially at the statistics of English pauperism to find that the quantity of paupers increases with every crisis, and diminishes with every revival of trade. Second, orphans and pauper children. These are candidates for the industrial reserve army, and are, in times of great prosperity, as 1860, e.g., speedily and in large numbers enrolled in the active army of laborers. Third, the demoralised and ragged, and those unable to work, chiefly people who succumb to their incapacity for adaptation, due to the division of labor; people who have passed the normal age of the laborer; the victims of industry, whose number increases with the increase of dangerous machinery, of mines, chemical works, etc., the mutilated, the sickly, the widows, etc. Pauperism is the hospital of the active labor-army and the dead weight of the industrial reserve army. Its production is included in that of the relative surplus-population . . . pauperism forms a condition of capitalist production, and of the capitalist development of wealth. It enters into the *faux frais* of capitalist production; but capital knows how to throw these, for the most part, from its own shoulders on to those of the working class and the lower middle class.[18]

The concept of "pauperization" leads us to consider the role of the "lumpenproletariat" in revolutionary struggle, a subject which has inspired great debate in the heart of the Puerto Rican liberation movement. Now is not the time to enter into that debate. Suffice it to point out that the category "lumpenproletariat," as described by Marx, requires, in each specific instance, an exhaustive study of its implications as a sector of the industrial urban proletariat.

We want likewise to emphasize the fact that "pauperism" and "lumpenproletariat" are not synonymous terms for Marx. Even though this is not the place to explain that important theoretical question, let it suffice to say that in no way is it fair to label the unemployed as "lumpen," although it cannot be denied that unemployment can push a person towards the ranks of the "lumpen." What we *are* interested in pointing out is the fact that capitalist—and, in our case, colonial—society produces and reproduces the conditions for pauperism, mass unemployment, marginalization and the "lumpenization" of great masses of our population—here and in the metropolis.

In a study by Harry Braverman,* to which we will refer further on, we are informed that the official list of indigents in England and Wales, with a total population estimated at 20,000,000, came to 971,433 in 1865. That was the equivalent of 4.6 percent of the total population. In the United States, on the other hand, if we take as our basis for analysis the welfare lists—14.8 million people in a population of 210.4 million in 1973—we will see that the figure is 7 percent of the total population. In Puerto Rico, the figure is much higher, especially when we take into account the fact that more than 70 percent of the population receives food stamps from the United States government.

That is pauperization, this reduction of great masses of people to a state of indigence.

Pauperism, of course, is ameliorated by all the mechanisms of the modern capitalist state, but it is still pauperism. Is pauperism not the rise in unemployment and underemployment to more than 30 percent of the labor force, the development of the "lumpenproletariat" in urban areas, and the terrible misfortune of those displaced by the process of industrialization, who have no other alternative than that of emigration? This pauperization places its victims in the almost despotic

*Harry Braverman, *Labor and Monopoly Capital* (New York: Monthly Review Press, 1974.)

dependency of the multiple programs of social security and benefits, welfare and now food stamps, intended to increase even more the psychological and sociological dependence of the great Puerto Rican masses.

All these factors have contributed to shape the general feature of the migratory and emigratory flow: the loss of more than one-third of the Puerto Rican population forced to abandon the national territory in search of salaried work. It could be argued—as do the defenders of the thesis of the "escape valve" theory—that no one *forces* peasants and workers to emigrate, that they do so freely, and that, if they consider it convenient to do so, their right to emigrate cannot be restricted. Nevertheless, we consider that it is *necessity* that serves as the principal motive for the massive emigration to the metropolis; and that the freedom not to do so in these cases is hollow and spurious. It is due to displacement and underdevelopment, unemployment and under-employment, and the *necessity* of having to provide for their means of subsistence, that our compatriots emigrate to the large U.S. cities and the agricultural fields of New England. It is not, therefore, a mere individual, voluntary act, but rather a real and objective process which takes power over the individual wills of those affected. It is a confirmation of Marx's thesis that "*In the social production of their existence, men . . . enter into definite relations,* which are independent of their will . . . "[19] Keeping that fact in mind, we will now proceed to discuss the particular forms that these relations of production have assumed in twentieth-century Puerto Rico.

According to this quote by Marx, *in the social production of their existence,* men enter into definite relations which are independent of their will. It is well worth the effort to stress this *social production of their existence,* since the process of production is one which has an eminently social, and not individual, character. In this social process of production, then, men enter into definite relations which take on a foreign and strange character for them. Structures created by men themselves resist change, producing the illusion and reality of a life of their own. That is why social change does not take place as a simple voluntaristic process, but rather within the context of certain deter-mined sociohistorical conditions that limit the scope and speed of the change. Marx expresses this clearly in the following observation: "Men make their own history, but they do not make it just as they please; they do not make it under circumstances chosen by themselves, but under circumstances directly encountered, given and transmitted from the past. The tradition of all the dead generations weighs like a nightmare on the brain of the living."[20]

Puerto Rican emigration should be seen and studied in light of this quote. Emigration has not been a fortuitous nor accidental process, as we have tried to show, nor has it been the product of mere individual decisions. No. It is the product of transformation in the material conditions of existence of Puerto Rican society, the product of changes not based on simple technological transformations, but rather on something much more profound: on the successive mutations through which a colonial society has had to pass, a society whose dependency has been multiplied extraordinarily in its passage from a sugar plantation economy to one of capitalist industrialization. It is a process over which we Puerto Ricans have not presided, especially if we consider it from two perspectives which constitute one and the same reality: from that of a society lacking the most elementary powers necessary to protect itself from massive economic penetration by imperialist interests; and from the point of view of an economic growth initiated and sustained under the stamp of dependent capitalism.

Under those circumstances, the transformations that have taken place in Puerto Rican economy and society during this century should be seen in the wider context of the strategy and tactics of imperialism which dominate and exploit in Latin America, and more specifically, the Caribbean. Neither the internal migratory movements nor the external emigration constitute a phenomenon peculiar to Puerto Rico, but rather one which can be seen with greater or lesser intensity in all the countries of the Caribbean.* It is not, therefore, an isolated fact, but a global phenomenon in which great masses of workers move continuously in accordance with fluctuations of the capitalist job-market.

The massive flow of Puerto Ricans, Dominicans, West Indians, and other Caribbean people to the United States is part of a process which should be traced to its roots: capitalist society and its transformations during the postwar period. In a recent study, Harry Braverman put his finger right on target in observing the following:

> In periods of rapid capital accumulation, such as that which has taken place throughout the capitalist world since World War II, the relative surplus

*See in this respect the judgment of Dr. George Beckford in the Colloquium on "Relaciones Internacionales y estructuras políticas en el Caribe," which took place in Mexico City in November, 1974. (Manuscript)

population which is the "natural" product of the capital accumulation process is supplemented with other sources of labor. In northern Europe and the United States, the capitalist economies have increasingly made use of the masses of former agricultural labor in the colonies and neocolonies. These masses are thrown off by the process of imperialist penetration itself, which has disrupted the traditional forms of labor and subsistence. They become available to capital as its own agricultural surplus labor (that part of the relative surplus population which Marx called the "latent" portion) is used up. As a result of this, the movement of labor has to some extent become internationalized, although still regulated in each country by government action in an attempt to make it conform to the national needs of capital. Thus Western Europe and the United States now draw upon a labor reservoir which extends in a broad band from India and Pakistan in the east across northern Africa and southernmost Europe all the way to the Caribbean and other portions of Latin America in the west. Indian, Pakistani, Turkish, Greek, Italian, African, Spanish, West Indian, and other workers supplement the indigenous underclass in northern Europe and make up its lowest layers. In the United States, the same role is occupied by Puerto Rican, Mexican. and other Latin American workers, who have been added to the pool of lowest-paid labor which is made up chiefly of black workers.[21]

As Braverman indicates, the process natural to the very development of capitalism, since with the Second World War, has led to the dislocation of the colonial and neocolonial economies and to the creation of a vast reserve industrial army at an international level. It is very interesting to note how Marx's description and analysis of nineteenth century English capitalist economy brings it to life for us today, but this time from a wider, more comprehensive perspective. (This also serves to explain why Malthus' ghost walks again among the ideologues of neocapitalism.)

Braverman's work could be substantiated with the figures in a United Nations Secretary General's report—the work of this international organization's Commission of Social Development—as well as by another report prepared by the United Nations Commission on Human Rights on the problems of discrimination against emigrant workers.

In the first report, the United Nation's Secretary General tells us: it is estimated that the total number of emigrants who worked *legally* in Western Europe was 7.3 million and with their dependents, 11.9 million. The total, including illegal emigrants, could go as high as 13 million, equivalent to the population of the Low Countries of Europe. The contracted work force in these cases is generally unskilled or semi-skilled in a proportion that exceeds 60 percent of the total of emigrant workers.

The same source makes the following observations about the origin and destination of the emigrants: there were 700,000 Algerians, 170,000 Moroccans and 100,000 Tunisians in France in 1971. In Belgium, the number for these three nationalities was 26,000; West Germany had 23,000 and the Low Countries 18,000.

In our hemisphere, according to the report, the principal emigration flow from the West Indies is to the United States and England. For example, the emigration from the West Indies to England went from about 1,000 per year around 1952 to 17,000 per year ten years later. After legislation was passed restricting the right of entry to England for citizens of the British Commonwealth, the flow stabilized at around 7,000 people a year. As for Latin America, the principal migratory movements are to Argentina and Venezuela; it is estimated that 1,600,000 people from Bolivia, Brazil, Chile, Paraguay and Uruguay emigrated to Argentina in 1969. There are also between 300,000 and 700,000 Colombian emigrants in Venezuela.[22]

It is useful to quote from another U.N. report which dramatizes the conditions of the migrant workers. The document is signed by Mme. Halina Warzazi and titled, "Exploitation of Labor Through Illicit and Clandestine Trafficing." Among other things, Mrs. Warzazi says the following:

> The migrant workers, irregardless of where they go, occupy the lowest rung of the socio-occupational ladder, simply because the majority of them are illiterate and because, when a developed country reaches a certain level of technological development its own workers abandon the inferior occupational levels, and foreign workers are recruited to compensate for this abandoning and to do the work refused by those workers born in the developed country . . . If we look to the future of the industrialized countries in relation to the migrant workers we will note that . . . Foreign labor makes possible the increase of the technological capacity of the country receiving the migrants at the same time as it reduces the cost of production per unit. Everything which the migrant workers produce, leaving to one side what they need for their own consumption, represents a net gain. If it were not for this work, construction of public buildings, common facilities and all works of infrastructure (dams, highways) in West Germany, the United Kingdom and France would be paralyzed. The mining industries, and iron and steel would be seriously affected, especially in Belgium and Luxembourg, and somewhat of the same thing would happen with the textile industries in Switzerland and the United Kingdom.[23]

In other words, the extraction of surplus value from migrant workers is what makes the German and Belgian "Economic Miracle" possible. We could say the same for the extremely important role of Black, Asian, Chicano, and Puerto Rican workers, etc., within U.S. capitalist society. They are the ones who supply and constitute the worst-paid labor force within that society. Therefore, capital accumulation in the United States, during its peak periods, is tightly connected to the Puerto Rican and Black labor force, as is the growth of the French economy tied to the recruiting of the Algerian labor force.

Puerto Rico does not constitute an exception to this reality. On the contrary, the Puerto Rican working class is in fact the object of a double exploitation that also has no geographic escape. This exploitation goes on both in Puerto Rico and in the metropolis, like the two faces of the same social reality. In Puerto Rico, under a system whose necessary consequences are unemployment, marginalization and emigration; and in the United States, under a capitalist society where racism assigns the Puerto Rican worker to the "bottom rung of the social ladder." The same is true for the Algerian in France or the Jamaican in England.

Hence the importance of a sociohistoric analysis of Puerto Rican emigration. Anything else would turn out to be a waste of time, a simple "ideological" (in the worst sense of the word) excursion.

We believe that the transformations suffered by Puerto Rican society during this century should be traced in like manner to their socioeconomic roots. To do otherwise, to reduce our society's transformations to mere changes in the ruling *technology,* suffers from the inability to see things as an *organic totality,* that is, it suffers from the defect of seeing technological transformation in abstraction from the rest of the changes which are carried out at the level of the entire community. The most simplistic definition of the problem—which is the one offered by the ideologues of "Fomento"—consists of reducing the sociohistoric Puerto Rican process to the simple equation of the passage of some agricultural structures to other, industrial kinds. In that case, the transformations suffered by our society during this century—but above all beginning with the post–World War II period— are seen simply as the "natural" process of "economic growth" the passage from an agricultural society to an urban and industrialized one. These same ideologues explain that emigration is the effect of the needs of a rapid economic transformation of our economic structures, which has the objective of eliminating poverty, unemployment and economic backwardness. Someone has to pay the price for progress, they tell us, and that someone is the Puerto Rican peasant and worker, forced to sell their labor power to foreign capitalists, or by default, to emigrate to the United States when they do not find work in Puerto Rico.

But the result of the program of "Fomento" seems today to be the antithesis of what its creators proposed to achieve: instead of economic growth, we have stagnation; instead of wealth, misery; instead of employment, unemployment. In order to understand what has happened, it is necessary to analyze the structural problems of the Puerto Rican economy during the last century.

In the first place, we should note that the consolidation of a plantation economy that revolved around the one-crop production of sugar cane was a process that covered the first four decades of this century. Its inevitable sequel was migration from the mountainous areas to the coastal areas where the sugar mills are found, and the formation of a vast rural proletariat, whose existence was determined by seasonal employment. The sugar season and "dead time" were the two sides of the same coin, and this contributed to the formation of a surplus work force, fertile soil for emigration to the cities or to the metropolis. On the other hand, a parallel process took place—the expropriation of the weak Puerto Rican bourgeoisie by the great U.S. sugar consortiums, a fact described graphically during the first decade of this century by Rosendo Matienzo Cintrón when he maintained: "Grandfather, landowner; Father, doctor; Son, *jornalero,*"* was the inevitable destiny of a social class in the process of disappearing. More recently, Professor Angel Quintero Rivera has helped confirm the validity of this description by that great Puerto Rican nationalist leader of the beginning of the 20th century.[24]

When the Second World War ended, the Partido Popular Democrático—which came into power in 1940—embarked on the program of the "Law of Industrial Incentives," better known as "Fomento Económico." "Fomento" is a process that can be briefly described in the following way: Puerto Rico must take up the road of industrialization, and also turn its back on agriculture. "Fomento Económico" would be a kind of experimental process, a flashy showcase where the "miracles" of free enterprise would be exhibited to all of Latin America. Our homeland would serve once again as "the bridge between the two great cultures of the hemisphere," only this time through the road of "economic development."

*Day laborer.

The first phase of the "Fomento" program—which we would place approximately between 1947 and 1960—is one built on the foundation of what its economists call "intensive labor industries," that is, medium or small businesses, with light machinery and with a high coefficient of workers. (An archetype of this enterprise was the needle industry.) Naturally, a process of this kind does not permit the absorption of manual labor which has been accustomed to agricultural work, and which does not have the training or necessary skills for the type of work required in the factories. As a result, there occurs a rapid process of migration to the urban centers, which serve as centers for light industries. In the same way, an exodus to the metropolis takes place when the displaced workers do not find work in the big cities of the Island. On the other hand, an urban industrial proletariat that revolves around manufacturing and construction is formed. We also witness the vigorous surge of the middle socioeconomic strata, who hold bureaucratic jobs in government and private enterprise while the ties of dependency between the Puerto Rican big bourgeoisie and United States industrial and finance capital are more strongly cemented.

The second phase of the "Fomento" Program goes from 1960 (approximately) up to today. It deals with transformation of the very structure of the Puerto Rican economy, as is implied by the passage from "intensive labor" businesses to those of "intensive capital." Businesses are established with a high coefficient of capital—especially of heavy machinery, as in the case of the petrochemical companies—and with a low coefficient of labor. The remainder of the agricultural sector is practically eliminated as a significant sector and the process of centering our economy on the petrochemical industry to an even greater degree hurls the working masses into the orbit of the unemployed. This dislocation and uprooting of the working class make unemployment and underemployment oscillate between 30 percent and 40 percent of the work force. The government itself has had to acknowledge this fact in a report on the Puerto Rican economy submitted by Governor Hernández Colón to U.S. President Ford in 1974.[25] At the same time, an exodus has already begun of those light industries which have used up all their tax exemptions and which today resort to the new "Fomento" programs of Haiti and the Dominican Republic. The shutting down of factories in the towns of the interior is having catastrophic effects. The profound crises that afflict the Puerto Rican economy are openly evident. The problems it confronts are structural in character and cannot be solved by simple reformist panaceas. As the degree of automation of the petrochemical businesses increases, so much greater will be the unemployment and misery of the working class.

The desperation which is spreading among the Puerto Rican colonial elite reflects the desperation spreading within the U.S. ruling class in the face of the profound crisis which is today rocking the foundations of the capitalist world. In its desperation, the Puerto Rican ruling class, which serves as intermediary for the interests of imperialism in Puerto Rico, is incapable of seeing beyond the preservation of the capitalist mode of production and it clings to it with all of its weak forces. Among the advice produced by this desperation, we will find emigration and mass sterilization as the answers to the crisis. Prisoners of their own creation, the leaders of Puerto Rican politics are trying to respond to big illnesses with grandiose cures, not caring whether the cures are worse than the diseases. This is how they are reacting to a situation that demands going to the roots of the disease as the only real way to arrive at a solution to this dilemma. But this would be too much to ask from leaders incapable of responding to anything but the interests of the system they defend. Therefore, the exploited classes, the working men and women, who suffer on their skins this process through which unemployment, pauperism or emigration are offered as the only alternatives, are those who ought to play the central role in the revolutionary process that will put an end to the false dilemma posed by the Puerto Rican colonialists.

An abstract law of population exists for plants and animals only, and only insofar as man has not interfered with them.

KARL MARX

2

EMIGRATION AND NEO-MALTHUSIANISM

Let us proceed from an incontestable demographic fact which Dr. José Luis Vázquez Calzada, one of our most distinguished demographers, describes as "one of the largest population exoduses registered by contemporary history." The magnitude of this exodus can be seen in the following statistics: between 1898 and 1944, approximately 90,000 people emigrated from Puerto Rico to the United States. During the 1940s, 150,000 Puerto Ricans emigrated; in the 1950s, 40,000. This leads Vázquez Calzada to claim that: "If we add to the total number of emigrants the number of children who would have been born to them had they remained on the Island, we arrive at the conclusion that, between 1940 and 1960, the Island lost around one million people as a result of this mass emigration."[1] Vázquez Calzada also indicates that during the 1950s, 70 percent of the emigrants were between the ages of 15 and 39.

Despite the fact that some 50,000 Puerto Ricans returned to Puerto Rico during the 1950s, and 253,212 during the 1960s, the facts show that we are clearly dealing with a massive emigration. During this same period, 586,636 Puerto Ricans emigrated to the United States, leaving a net emigration balance of 253,212 (in the 1960's).[2] The full picture shows that within the period from 1945 to today, more than half a million Puerto Ricans have emigrated to the metropolis and settled there. This helps explain why there are, conservatively speaking, a grand total of one and a half million Puerto Ricans on U.S. soil, and probably closer to two million if we also count third generation emigrant *Boricuas*.

One-third of the Puerto Rican population is found outside of the national territory and this has profound consequences not only for the destiny of Puerto Rico as a Spanish-speaking country but also for the development of the struggle for independence and socialism among our people.

The cultural and political consequences resulting from these demographic changes demand our most careful attention, and will be discussed later.

First of all, however, we would like to define how the Puerto Rican ruling class has perceived the emigrant exodus as well as examine the measures they have tried to implement in order to solve the problem. We are also interested in knowing the ruling class' rationalizations of the alleged necessity of the exodus. In other words, we want to see—once we have examined the historical-structural transformations that have produced and reproduced the emigration problem—what arguments are used by the defenders of the colonial-capitalist mode of production when these defenders try to offer *their* conception of the causes and effects of emigration.

Let us begin with what we might call the ideology—we use the term in its Marxist sense—of those who conclude that Puerto Rican emigration has been "inevitable," that Puerto Ricans have emigrated in great numbers to the United States because they were convinced of the prospects of better and fuller horizons in the heart of a new "promised land." According to this thesis, emigration has had a purely voluntary character, since Puerto Ricans, rather than having been *forced* to emigrate, have done so in the exercise of their own free will. Given this "reality," one has then to accept emigration as a *fait accompli;* accepting that there are no alternatives given the smallness of the Island, its population density and its high rate of unemployment and underemployment. In other words, for the ideologues of mass emigration, it is essentially a remedy—disagreeable but necessary—for solving other social problems of great importance that afflict us. Perhaps the best example of what we mean can be found in an editorial in the newspaper, *El Nuevo Día* (February 27, 1974), where many of the points of view just expressed are brought together and the "inevitability" of Puerto Rican emigration is accepted. It is important to point out that although this newspaper represents the position of the Partido Nuevo Progresista (New Progressive Party)—of annexationist tendencies—its criteria transcend party lines and form part of a world-view prevalent among the class that clings to colonial power in Puerto Rico. Therefore, we quote this editorial in its entirety:

> In short and long terms, the most serious problem of Puerto Rico is its somber population density. Judging from the declarations of Secretary of Natural Resources, Cruz A. Matos, in a symposium held at the University of Puerto Rico, the population density of our Island is presently 875 people per square mile, resulting in a total population of 2,905,625 in comparison with the 2,712,033 inhabitants which was the official figure of the federal census of April, 1970. Taking these figures as a base, we can calculate that in 1980 our Island will have 3,200,000 inhabitants.
>
> One will therefore see that since Puerto Rican life already demands more living space, one will have to look for a livelihood in the lands of promise of the American world. The problem also raises the inescapable obligation of preparing the Puerto Rican with the necessary working and professional skills and with the command of other languages, so that he might make a living and progress economically and competitively in the new lands.
>
> The lands which attract are, of course, those of the United States of America, where we can advantageously develop in the economic, social and political orders, because we are already citizens, and the advantage will be greater if in our schools we include not only the command of English, but also the acquisition of disciplines with high economic yield.
>
> And other lands of promise might also be immense Brazil or any other country of South or Central America.
>
> Concurrently, and as a fixed policy of all our governments, we are obliged to increase the Island's production on all levels, as an imperative patriotic duty.
>
> As we see it, it will be an inevitable exodus, and many Puerto Ricans will have to get used to carrying their small homeland, as Gautier Benítez would say, "like the memory of a profound love," in their nostalgia and affection, and they will also have to get used to giving practical application to the Latin aphorism *ubi bene, ibi patria*—wherever one is well, there too is the homeland.

The principal ideological mouthpiece of the other colonial party, the Partido Popular Democrático (Popular Democratic Party), tells us the same thing with even greater impudence. We are referring naturally to that ineffable homonym of Chile's *El Mercurio,* San Juan's *El Mundo,* which on June 22, 1975, editorialized:

> We Puerto Ricans ought to be profoundly concerned with the rising change in the migratory tendency. Contrary to what has been going on for decades, more of our countrymen are returning to the Island than leaving it.
>
> In the face of this turn of events, which characterizes today's migratory

movement, the importance of the massive exodus of Puerto Ricans to the United States, particularly in the 1950's and 1960's, becomes even more significant for us than before. Those who return find many jobs and aggravate the unemployment problem in the country. Now that these brothers are returning perhaps we will be able to see, in all its crude reality, the enormous, snowballing problem of overpopulation that we are faced with in this small piece of land we call Puerto Rico.

There are almost two million Puerto Ricans in the United States, of whom many will return to the Island sooner or later. It is easy to imagine what would occur if all those Puerto Ricans who live in the United States decided to return to Puerto Rico. *And it is easy to calculate what would have happened with our progress if they had never abandoned the Island to go to the United States in search of work.*

The migratory current from the Island to the Continent prevented the brutal growth of unemployment in Puerto Rico. The Puerto Rican worker in the United States not only aided himself and his family on the Island, but he also received a better education and skills with which to obtain better salaries in an industrialized society like ours. Many of them are going to come back, we don't know how many, but the number is not important, because in any case this becomes an additional argument for Puerto Rico to take on more drastic methods of birth control.

We are already more than three million here. And another two million over there. From the human and ecological points of view, Puerto Rico is rapidly becoming a place where one will not be able to live.

This thesis, which is, to our mind, representative of a whole conception of the economic development of Puerto Rico within the context of its relation to the United States, has been endorsed on multiple occasions by the Administrator of Fomento Económico, Mr. Teodoro Moscoso. Mr. Moscoso, nevertheless, has been more explicit than the editors of *El Nuevo Día* and *El Mundo,* and in several published declarations (*El Mundo,* April 4, 1974) seeks to tie the emigration problem to the variables of unemployment and a high birth rate. Therefore, in the dispatch cited above, Mr. Moscoso admits that the rate of unemployment is officially 12 percent, although the real rate could be as high as 30 percent. But the problem of unemployment, he adds, will not be solved if something is not done to control birth in Puerto Rico. Here, then, is the complement of Puerto Rican emigration: population control. Both phenomena march hand in hand as part of the strategy for the development of Puerto Rico designed by "Fomento Económico."

What has been quoted thus far could be taken as a simple position of a newspaper or of a public functionary. But when we receive a report from a "Subcommittee of the Governor of Puerto Rico" about "work, educational and training opportunities," signed by none other than Dr. Luis Silva Recio, Secretary of Labor; Mr. Teodoro Moscoso, Administrator of Fomento Económico; Dr. Ramón A. Cruz, Secretary of Public Education; Dr. Amador Cobas, President of the University of Puerto Rico, and the team of technicians of the Planning Board and Department of the Budget, we face a very different kind of reality. We are dealing with nothing less than a statement about the standards that should guide the government of the "Free Associated State" in matters of employment, education, and so on. The report, submitted to the Governor in November, 1973, could not be more explicit in its conclusions and recommendations:

> We can conclude from the lessons of history of the last decades that: (1) the unemployment problem has been, continues to be and will be for many years one of the fundamental economic problems of Puerto Rico; (2) the government has tried to solve the unemployment problem through the creation of the most jobs possible and, indirectly, through the reduction of the work force, making a limited and a somewhat concealed effort to reduce the birth rate; (3) the emigration of the unemployed who voluntarily have decided to leave, has constituted the *escape valve* (author's, emphasis) that has prevented unemployment from acquiring catastrophic proportions. The projections of the Planning Board, based on the natural growth of population, emigration and rates of participation, state that the growth of the work force will average 28,000 people annually from 1975 to 1985. Therefore, if we want to reach our goal of 5% unemployment here in 1985, we will have to substantially change the present tendencies with respect to supply and demand of jobs. In order to achieve this, the government will have to draw up a plan of action that will produce a reduction in job demand by means of a series of measures related to: (1) a migration program that results in a lesser influx of people returning to Puerto Rico and possibly a greater flow out of Puerto Rico; (2) an active program of keeping the greatest possible number of young people in the school system. The birth control program, which is also urgent and necessary, would come to have an effect on the work force after 1985.[3]

We should note the term "escape valve" in the present context. This is doubtlessly a metaphor whose point of reference seems to be a pressure cooker about to explode. The pressure cooker in question is Puerto Rico, which threatens to blow up because of an excess of accumulated gas—the population. The escape valve—emigration—will go on being the antidetonator. But emigration alone is not enough. It is also necessary to reduce population growth as much as possible.

In the quoted report, we are given the following statistics: of the 485,948 women of child-rearing age in Puerto Rico, excepting the municipality of San Juan, 160,365 are sterilized. This leaves a *"potential clientele"* (the words of the report) of 325,585 women, of whom around 75,000 are already taking advantage of the medical and contraceptive services of the Department of Health and the Puerto Rican Association of Family Welfare. In the same report, we discover that "almost 33% of the female population of child-rearing age are sterilized." But this is not enough, since we have seen that it is still necessary to sterilize this "potential clientele."

In order to implement this plan, the government of the "Commonwealth of Puerto Rico" has established an undersecretary for "Family Planning," presently headed by Dr. Antonio Silva Iglesias.

Dr. Silva Iglesias has taken up his task as supreme "family planner" of Puerto Rico with the fervor of a crusader. According to his plans, there ought to be a minimum of 25 voluntary sterilization centers established throughout the Island, in each of which, "in principle a total of 10 sterilizations would be performed per week." Dr. Silva Iglesia's goal is the sterilization of some 5,000 Puerto Rican women a month, with the eventual objective of arriving at zero population growth. In his own words, the Family Planning program "has as its chief objective the reduction of the rate of population growth so as to bring about a better socio-economic balance. Toward those ends and voluntarily, the program will provide medical and educational services offered to reduce the birth rate so as to result in zero population growth."[4] The criterium for carrying out the sterilizations is only the alleged consent of the patient. But Dr. Silva has a more ambitious goal. Up to now, he states, sterilization has been a costly surgical operation, which explains why 70 percent of sterilized women are in high income brackets. Therefore, the "Family Planning" program is interested in the poor women of Puerto Rico, or in Dr. Silva's words: "it seems to me that a person of limited resources and of a large family ought to be sterilized."[5] There is no need to go on. It is clear that we are dealing with a neo-Malthusian plan for the massive sterilization of proletarian and peasant Puerto Rican women.

Nothing reveals better the mentality of the director of "Family Planning" than his response to being asked whether or not these sterilization programs conflicted with the affluence of Cuban exiles in Puerto Rico, whose total number is approximated at 50,000. With his typical candor, Dr. Silva Iglesias stated: "The Cuban immigration has not been dangerous in economic terms because those who have arrived from Cuba for the most part are well educated. *The return of the Puerto Ricans living in the United States would indeed be dangerous.* (Author's emphasis) And presently, more Puerto Ricans are settling in the Island than in the United States."[6]

We have come around full circle. We are again faced with Puerto Rican emigration, but now seen as a "danger" because it is now a case of our compatriots who might decide to return to their homeland. Once again, here is clearly the inextricable relationship between emigration, unemployment, over-population and birth control, all seen, not as isolated social phenomena, but rather as integral parts of that "organic totality" which is twentieth-century Puerto Rican society.

As you can see, the "escape valve" is not sufficient as an antidote for the "population explosion." It is also necessary that the emigrants not return to Puerto Rico. To continue with the use of "explosive" images: it is a matter of hurling out of the national territory thousands and thousands of Puerto Ricans—the immense majority of whom are unemployed—with the vigilant and expressed hope that they will never return to settle on Puerto Rican soil. But even this is not enough. It does not suffice for proletarian and peasant Puerto Ricans to go to the metropolis. The population growth of the people in Puerto Rico should be reduced to zero. As the reader will see, this represents an inverted causality, which claims that the existing unemployment in Puerto Rico does not relate to the structural changes which have taken place in the Puerto Rican economy during the last thirty-some-odd years, but rather is the primary effect of excessive population growth. And great cures are prescribed for great ills. We will wipe out massive unemployment through massive emigration and massive sterilization. These "cures" obviously mean that Malthus' ghost has been revived by the ideologues of imperialism in an attempt to ward off the prevailing presence of Marx.

In truth, the Puerto Rican ideologues of massive emigration and neo-Malthusianism simply repeat the well-known arguments related to the world "population explosion" and its catastrophic consequences. Catastrophic, to be sure, for a capitalist country—like the United States—which contains only five percent of the world population while enjoying more than fifty percent of the earth's wealth. But there is more. We are referring to an entire ideology dealing with the causes of "economic anti-development and development," which is none other than W. W. Rostow's well-known thesis of the stages of economic growth. When one outlines this thesis with all its corollaries, the ideologues of colonial capitalism speak of Puerto Rico as if it were an industrially developed country and they therefore refuse to see us as part of the exploited and underdeveloped peoples of the Third World. But, at the same time, they find themselves forced to admit that this economic growth is not self-sustaining and that their plans for economic development depend on the massive influx of foreign capital, attracted by tax exemptions, low salaries and an abundant labor supply. When this influx is paralyzed, the false development will become paralyzed as well.

It is essential to point out that such arguments are not only fatalistic—most of the time a product of a colonialist mentality with no faith in the people—but also false. We see this at both world and national levels. To begin with, let us look at the problem from the point of view of our national reality.

According to the prophets of fatalism, our society is eternally condemned to underdevelopment and poverty. Hence, our only salvation is found in population control, emigration and the importation of capital, since we are a small country, overpopulated and lacking in natural resources. Given this inflexible reality, all we can do is resign ourselves to our fate and increase more and more our dependence on U.S. capitalism. It is of little importance that deposits of copper and other minerals have been discovered, whose value is approximated in the billions of dollars; that there is evidence of the existence of petroleum in our subsoil; that we have an exceptional future in the technological exploitation of agriculture—especially sugar cane. None of this is important to those who still repeat that we lack natural resources, that we are small and overpopulated, and so on.

It is clear that Puerto Rico has a high population density. But population density is not automatically the primary determinant of poverty and unemployment. Compare the population densities of Haiti and Holland. We immediately see that Haiti is an underdeveloped country with a low population density, while Holland is a highly industrialized capitalist country with a high population density. The difference between the two is not to be found simply in population density, but in the economic bases of development of both countries. The ideologues of neo-Malthusianism are forced to look for new

arguments when confronted with these realities. What they overlook—
very conveniently, of course—is the essential difference between the
development of the rich capitalist countries and the *anti*development
from which the poor countries of the Third World systematically
suffer.[7]

Paul Singer clarifies the problem for us even more when he writes:

> Therefore, one cannot study development as an historical process which
> begins with the Industrial Revolution in England and obeys the same laws
> since then. Development is the structural transformation of the national
> economies which are industrializing in a world shaped by colonial revolu-
> tion, not only by its successes, but also by its insufficiencies: in a world in
> which political independence combines with economic dependence and
> where the breaking with the international division of traditional work is
> much more painful and risky than the breaking with the political bonds of
> dependence. To consider such processes as identical—processes which are
> not only different, but, to a certain point, opposite—prevents appreciation
> of their innermost workings.[8]

Seen in this way, the problem presented acquires other hidden
dimensions for neo-Malthusianism. The root of Puerto Rico's unemployment and underdevelopment ought to be sought in the relationship
between the colonial society, the capitalist metropolis and the capitalist
division of world labor. The definitive bankruptcy of "Fomento" is
nothing more than the culmination of the bankruptcy of a strategy for
development, whose fragile foundations gave way as soon as the first
serious crisis of world capitalism occurred after the Great Depression.

It would be shortsighted, nevertheless, if we do not see the global
character of neo-Malthusianism as the ideology and strategy of imperialism in its growing confrontation with the raw material producing
countries of the Third World which today claim control of their natural
resources.[9] (The same thing can be said for the strategy of U.S.
monopoly capital, which seeks to limit population growth of Blacks,
Puerto Ricans, Chicanos, and other nationally oppressed groups,
within its own boundaries.) All this forms part of the world-view of the
ideologues of imperialism with respect to worldwide counterrevolu-
tion. Puerto Rico is one more chip on the table, but an important chip.

Actually, the neo-Malthusian thesis in its various versions is a
prescription for attempting to detain the world revolutionary process.
Just as Malthus himself would have done in his day, this ideology is
directed against population growth, and what this growth represents in
revolutionary potential. Regarding this, Samir Amin tells us:

In reality, the worldwide campaign to limit births in the Third World expresses the fears of the developed world, faced with the danger of a reshuffling of the international order by the peoples who are its primary victims. In the last instance, the development of the spontaneous tendencies of the present system would demand the reduction of the periphery population. The contemporary technological and scientific revolution, with the limits of this system, actually excludes the perspective of a productive employment of the marginal masses of the periphery. On the other hand, the literature referring to the "environment" makes Westerners slowly aware of the rhythm to which they exploit natural resources not only of their own countries but of the entire planet. If the masses of the Third World countries divert this exploitation of natural resources and place them at their own service, the functioning conditions of the central capitalist system would be overturned.[10]

The ideologues of emigration and neo-Malthusianism in Puerto Rico identify with the bourgeoisie of the capitalist countries, and express the class antagonisms that underlie their ideology in the same way. The Puerto Rican intermediary bourgeoisie wants to continue profiting from its privileged relationship—notwithstanding a subordinate one—with the metropolis, by promoting the exportation of a cheap labor force while it proceeds to cut the Fallopian tubes of an ever-increasing number of Puerto Rican women. With these measures they hope to ward off the crisis which becomes deeper every day.

These measures, however, are confronting a growing resistance by those victims who find themselves forced to suffer them. The structural contradictions of the Puerto Rican economy dependent on the metropolis sharpen class struggle and increasingly plunge us into poverty. The options of the colonial system in the face of the crisis are being progressively reduced. But none of this seems to perturb the colonial government which continues, undaunted, to pursue its old and often discredited panaceas. Because of this, it is becoming more and more urgent to expose the ideologues of emigration and neo-Malthusianism so as to establish the historical responsibilities for these crimes committed against our people.

Nothing that we have said so far should be interpreted as meaning that we oppose family planning. What we do oppose is that such planning should utilize the most irreversible and drastic method of all— that of mass sterilization—as a kind of panacea for all our social problems. True family planning must be conceived as part of world-wide social planning. From this point of view, this kind of planning is *not* in conflict with socialism, in fact, it can only be implemented within the bounds of a socialist society. It is precisely in a society such as ours, where true social planning does not exist, that "family planning" acquires the Orwellian characteristic of being the direct opposite of what its name suggests. That is why the apocalyptic prophets of the "population catastrophe" appear in our country to be desperate men, hungry to turn the country into a combination of geriatric hospital and barren women.[11]

It is precisely the study of demographic growth which ends up destroying all these apocalyptic visions of "population catastrophe." In fact, the most recent scientific analyses completely invalidate the above interpretation. Demographic growth must be seen in its fullest context in a *human society*. Dr. Barry Commoner, Director of the Center for the Biology of Natural Systems of the University of Washington in St. Louis, and member of the Board of Directors of Scientists helps put things in their proper perspective when he writes:

> ... there is a kind of critical standard of living which, if achieved, can lead to a rapid reduction in birthrate and an approach to a balanced population.

> Thus, in human societies, there is a built-in control on population size: If the standard of living, which initiates the rise in population, *continues* to increase, the population eventually begins to level off. This self-regulating process begins with a population in balance, but at a high death rate and low standard of living. It then progresses toward a population which is larger, but once more in balance, at a low death rate and a high standard of living.

> The chief reason for the rapid rise in population in developing countries is that this basic condition has not been met. The explanation is a fact about developing countries which is often forgotten—that they were recently, and in the economic sense often still remain, colonies of more developed countries. In the colonial period, western nations introduced improved living conditions (roads, communications, engineering, agriculture and medical services) as part of their campaign to increase the labor force needed to exploit the colony's natural resources. This increase in living standards initiated the first phase of the demographic transition.

> But most of the resultant wealth did not remain in the colony. As a result, the second (or population-balancing) phase of the demographic transition could not take place. Instead the wealth produced in the colony was largely diverted to the advanced nation—where it helped that country achieve for itself the second phase of the demographic transition. Thus colonialism involves a kind of demographic parasitism: The second, population-balancing phase of the demographic transition in the advanced country is fed by the suppression of that same phase in the colony.[12]

This is the focus which ought to prevail among the apostles of the improperly titled "Family Planning" in Puerto Rico. But that would be too much to ask of those who are bound to the imperialist world-view of demographic growth.

The ideologues of neo-Malthusianism and massive emigration have attempted to offer rationalizations for the social practices they use against Puerto Rican national integrity. The system itself, whose flagrant injustices they attempt to cover up, is passing through the most profound crisis of its history. In this context, colonialist ideology becomes shrill and hysterical. Having lost the bases of its spurious legitimacy, its ideologues are left with no other recourse but to appeal to naked power and brute force. They are not yet capable of sweetening the pill. Reality does not permit this. They are now limited to justifying the unjustifiable, as a last resort born of desperation. These are the bitter fruits of the ideologues of an economically, morally and spiritually bankrupt system, like the one we Puerto Ricans are forced to live in at this historic moment.

The mode of production of material life conditions the process of social, political and intellectual life in general. It is not men's consciousness which determines their existence; but rather their social existence is what determines their consciousness.

KARL MARX

3

A BRIEF RETROSPECTIVE

The first Puerto Rican emigrations to the United States begin before the military occupation of Puerto Rico by U.S. troops. These first emigrants were for the most part, political exiles: Puerto Rican revolutionaries who were conspiring on U.S. territory to break once and for all with the yoke of Spanish colonialism. Puerto Rican and Cuban exiles founded the famous Partido Revolucionario Cubano (Cuban Revolutionary Party), over whose Puerto Rican section honorarily presided the Father of our Homeland, Dr. Ramón Emeterio Betances. José Martí was to become the leader and inspirer of that liberation party and Betances one of its greatest standard-bearers.[1]

But it is with the U.S. occupation of the Island in 1898 that the emigratory phenomenon materialized in all its helplessness. The ideologues of colonial history have tried to attribute the economic crisis that struck the Island soon after the invasion to the devastating effects of the hurricane known as San Ciriaco (1899). Without a doubt, this hurricane inflicted serious losses on *Boricuan* agriculture, but the most recent studies show that there were other, even more devastating causes that explain the systematic process of expropriation of Puerto Rican landlords, which we observe from that moment on. I am referring to three measures taken by the Military Governor, Guy V. Henry (December, 1898, to May, 1899), namely: the freezing of long and short-term credit; the devaluation of the Puerto Rican *peso;* and land price-fixing. The economists José A. Herrero, Víctor Sánchez Cardona and Elías Gutiérrez tell us in reference to these measures:

The devaluation produced a strong reduction in the monetary supply. This reduction and credit-freezing caused serious difficulties in obtaining the money required to pay for normal business costs. The fact that revenues were only obtained after the harvest was sold created great pressure. The farmers and landlords saw themselves forced therefore to liquidate all or part of their property in order to obtain the money they needed.

It is not surprising therefore that a great number of farmers and landlords were ruined when, unable to resort to credit, they saw themselves forced to sell their lands at the low prices fixed by Henry. Moreover, the only buyers in the market were those who had dollars; these were either North American corporations, or Puerto Rican corporations linked to commerce with the United States. That is why it becomes easy to understand how, in the short span of four years, four North American corporations that were to be dedicated to sugar production came to control directly 70,000 *cuerdas** of agricultural land.[2]

With this political economy, the first chapter of the economic and political domination of our homeland by U.S. imperialism begins. The basis is thereby established to implant an economy centered on the great sugar plantations. In the international capitalist division of labor, the Caribbean—but especially the Antilles—was made to assume the role of supplier of tropical products, especially sugar cane. The bankruptcy of the landlords engaging in coffee and tobacco cultivation was to be only a matter of time. It is this restructuring of the Puerto Rican economy, under the new imperialist stamp, which allows us to see with greater clarity in what way thousands of Puerto Rican workers were to be hurled into unemployment and pauperism, and at the same time made the easy preys of emigration. The dislocation of the Puerto Rican economy, which began in all its severity in 1898, is yet to be studied with the profundity that the subject deserves. We are absolutely certain that a short time after the occupation, recruiters from the great sugar plantations in Hawaii came to Puerto Rico in search of workers. Their objective was to contract Puerto Rican *braceros* who were able and fit to work on those plantations. Emigration at that moment was not limited to Hawaii; there were also emigrations, or emigration attempts, to Cuba, the Dominican Republic, Yucatan, and Panama during the first five years of U.S. domination. That this emigratory movement was important can be concluded from Colonial Governor Allen's First Annual Report in 1910. He says:

*In Puerto Rico, a *cuerda* is a land surface measurement equivalent to 3.929 square meters.

Henceforth, emigration has been almost unknown . . . But particularly since the hurricane of San Ciriaco some of the poorer class of laborers have found it difficult to procure the means of a livelihood . . . In this state of affairs, the emigration agent found an excellent field for his enterprise. He penetrated the rural districts and offered golden inducements to these simple folk to travel and see foreign lands. Laborers are wanted in Hawaii to work in the sugar fields, and in Cuba for the iron mines. Good wages are offered, and many are persuaded to emigrate. So they crowd the seaport towns of Ponce, Mayaguez and Guanica. Very few embark at San Juan . . . Most of the emigrants are of the very poorest class of laborers, many of them without a box or a bundle or anything whatever more than the scanty apparel in which they stand upon the wharves. Very few of them have the least rudiments of education. In other words, these emigrants comprise the least desirable elements of this people.

Most of them have gone to Honolulu, some thousands have gone to Cuba, and a few to Santo Domingo . . . Porto Rico has plenty of laborers and poor people generally.[3]

The statistics that Igualdad Iglesias de Pagán presents concerning emigration to Hawaii affirmed that, in the short period between November, 1900 and August, 1901, a total of 5,303 Puerto Rican workers emigrated to Hawaii.[4] This emigration caused great concern among Puerto Rican workers at the beginning of the century. The workers' leaders Ramón Romero Rosa, José Ferrer y Ferrer, Eduardo Conde and Saturnino Dones protested vehemently before the colonial authorities, attacking the practice. They said:

Due to the shocking misery that prevails in our countryside; due to the hunger that exists in the homes of the poor *jíbaros,* and to the absolute lack of work, a hideous crime is being committed in Puerto Rico, a crime that denigrates and vilifies us.

In that crime, which can be called treasonous to humanity, a vile commercial traffic is carried out with our brothers, the rural proletariat, leading and contracting us to the fatal regions of Hawaii and Ecuador . . .

And were it to continue in this way, honorable citizens, shortly the Puerto Rican working people will have disappeared, buried forever in those countries, to which misery, hunger and deceit are taking them.[5]

Later studies show that the Puerto Rican population in Hawaii rose to some 10,000 people.[6] Our knowledge of the experiences of these compatriots is rather fragmentary. Together with the emigration to Saint Croix, which we will discuss later on, *Boricuan* emigration to Hawaii has been, without doubt, one of the most important recorded, before the massive emigration to the United States during the postwar period.

We need to emphasize the fact that the Puerto Rican economy, which was centered during the first four decades of this century in the *latifundio* one-crop production of sugar cane, was of a seasonal nature. This produced the fatal "dead time" for the sugar workers. During the period between harvests, Puerto Rican workers had to look for means of subsistence for themselves and their families. When opportunities like going to work in Hawaii or California appeared, desperation dragged them into exile, families and all. We have to take into consideration, that at that time, great conveniences of communication and transportation which today exist between Puerto Rico and the metropolis did not exist, and this made the emigratory flow difficult, or at least tended to reduce it considerably.

However, despite this, considerable parallels do exist between the situation then and now. A concrete example is the job offers of the Yankee sugar companies based in Hawaii. The offers could not have been more attractive: good salaries, adequate housing, good working conditions, etc. That was the bait until the Puerto Rican emigrants actually set foot on the shores of their destination. Then, everything disappeared. The naked face of exploitation was bared, as was the defenselessness of the Puerto Rican workers.

The promotion of emigration as the solution to Puerto Rico's problems was suggested again in 1914 by Colonial Governor Yager, provoking the angered response of José de Diego in an article entitled "The displacement." De Diego says:

> It has happened and still happens in the world that, upon the clashing of arms, an army levels a country, burns, kills, throws out of their homeland those who have defended it with sublime courage; but, then, in peace, through an agreement, coldly, premeditatively, the act of taking men from their homeland because they cannot "earn a living," this is the latest phenomenon, which the writers of international law, sociology, anthropology and all physical and moral sciences should record for future books.

> Why are there "so many of them"? Here you have, in these ingenuous words, the idea that Puerto Ricans are in the way in Puerto Rico, that the density of our population—the rampart that resists the destruction of our personality and our race—should be destroyed . . .[7]

That the emigratory question was the cause of concern for the colonial authorities is shown by the fact that the Legislative Assembly, on May 29, 1919, passed Law Number 19 "For the regulation of emigrations in Puerto Rico and for other objectives." This Law conferred authority to the Commissioner of Agriculture and Labor to understand "in all aspects everything concerning emigrations of workers in Puerto Rico." This commissioner would also have the power to investigate, inspect, intervene and regulate the propositions, promises, conditions and offers made to native workers in cases of emigration; and to manage, subscribe and see to it that formulated contracts were fulfilled, either by natural or juridical persons residing in or outside of Puerto Rico, be it in any state of the American union or foreign states; and to be attentive that stability or repatriation be guaranteed for all workers found outside of the Island.

The government of Puerto Rico explicitly declared that the protection of this law would not be extended to those who emigrated without a contract, and it disposed penalties for the least serious transgression of this Law. (The Law was then amended by Law 54 on May 1, 1936, and subsequently repealed by Law 89 on May 9, 1947.)

In 1926, Law 19 was to be put to the test. Let us recall the historic moment: in 1924, the United States restricted immigration on clearly racist and discriminatory grounds. This legislation, which was in effect up until 1965, "was specifically designed to favor white, Anglo-Saxon northern European immigrants and stem what was seen as a tide of Eastern European Jews, Slavs, and Italians . . . The 1924 law was even tougher on Orientals than on Eastern and Southern Europeans."[8]

A sudden shortage of manpower was created in the United States, especially a labor force for agricultural work. In the face of the shortage of manpower, the farmers cast their eyes toward Puerto Rico. This provided the scenario for one of the most pathetic episodes in the history of our homeland.

On August 28, 1926, the first announcement of the Arizona Cotton Growers Association appeared in the national press. The announcement read as follows:

An expedition of families of workers is being organized for the state of Arizona, United States. Single people will not be accepted. The contracts have been reviewed and approved by the Governor of Puerto Rico in accordance with the Laws of the country.

Spanish is spoken there; the Catholic religion is predominant; the climate is the same as Puerto Rico's and education is free and compulsory; the work will be permanent, general agricultural in character, although we specialize in cotton, melons, and vegetables. We have a workers compensation law. There will be adequate work for women . . . The minimum [day's wage] will be $2.00 daily. The ability of the worker will help him raise that wage. A house will be given free of charge. Each employer will be responsible for providing medical assistance.[9]

The offer immediately provoked an unprecedented movement among the workers of Puerto Rico. Hundreds and perhaps thousands of Puerto Ricans headed for the port of San Juan with their families on the stipulated date for the first trip to Arizona. Due to the fact that the boat was two days late, those who arrived in San Juan from the rural areas of the Island had to sleep without shelter or in railroad cars. A reporter captured the mood of several of the emigrants. Vicente Ramos, of Aguadilla, said, "If I had the money I'd head right now for my village. This is horrible. We are suffering bitterly. They promised us good services and in reality they're treating us like dogs." And Rufino Torres, from the same municipality, said, "I sold all my furniture, even a double bed. I have had to sleep two nights in this filthy railroad car!"[10]

While this was going on in the railroad area bordering the port of San Juan, the reporter interviewed a Mr. Mortenson in his office, one of the agents of the cotton company, and he asked him if it were true that Puerto Ricans were taken to Arizona to serve as strike-breakers. The answer of this Mr. Mortenson does not require any additional comment:

> You can confirm categorically that there is no strike of any kind in Arizona. Since 1913 not one protest movement on the part of workers has been registered. Emigration serves a different purpose. We need around 4,000 men. In Puerto Rico we'll get 1,500; the rest we'll take from California and Mexico.[11]

The *Boricuas* subjected to these ordeals on that September 9th finally set sail for the state of Arizona. Much later Carey MacWilliams wrote what took place:

> Under the pretext of a continuing "labor shortage," the Arizona Cotton Growers Association, in 1926, arranged with the Bureau of Insular Affairs of the Department of Interior to import 1,500 Puerto Ricans. The adventure was ill-fated from the start. On the day the first boatload sailed from San Juan, 6,000 Puerto Ricans, starving for work, clamored about the port demanding a chance to board the ship. "Rioting followed; . . . Most of those who sailed were Negroes, ill adapted to the new environment." . . . In Arizona the Puerto Ricans "could not be speeded up to the point where they could pick enough cotton to make a living. They soon became public charges."

> The labor scouts who had recruited these workers had grossly misrepresented conditions in Arizona. Workers were told that houses with "electric lights" were furnished, and that wages were high. When they discovered that they had been deceived, they staged a minor rebellion. Less than 50 per cent

remained in the fields; the others deserted the camps and marched into Phoenix . . . When the Governor called upon the cotton growers for an explanation, they suggested that the city and county adopt strict ordinances against "loitering." If this action was taken, they said, "we will have no difficulty in holding the supply of unskilled labor on the ranches." By the following season, 90 per cent of the Puerto Ricans had disappeared; they had "scattered like clouds." No one knows just where they went or what happened to them; but they were not returned to Puerto Rico.[12]

The rebellion of Puerto Ricans who emigrated to Arizona in 1926 is one of so many episodes in our history of exploitation—high-sounding promises which later vanish into thin air. That is why the now familiar words of colonial functionaries become twice as interesting, in what they reveal to us about the present-day situation of the emigrants. Dr. Carlos E. Chardón, at that time Commissioner of Agriculture and Labor, would pronounce a statement we have heard many times since, namely, that "this movement has not been sponsored nor encouraged by us. All we have done is lend our cooperation which we could not deny them and which we were compelled to offer them by the statute that regulates the relations between Puerto Rico and the national territory."[13]

Nevertheless, a letter from the migrant worker Angel Hernández López, from Scottsdale, Arizona, to his mother said:

Here there aren't any such cotton companies like they told us there'd be in Puerto Rico before we left. We've been sold. When we arrived, there were more than a hundred cars waiting for us. To send us different places. Each American grabbed several families for his farm. Those of us who have come here will die of old age and won't see one another again. The American who went to Puerto Rico to recruit for emigration went to sell us here to others. He deceived us miserably since we haven't found any cotton company.[14]

Dr. Nieves Falcón's recent book offers similar burning testimony of farmworker accounts of barely two years ago. And the response from today's Secretary of Labor is practically identical to the one offered by the Secretary of Labor in office in 1926.

The passage of the new U.S. Law of 1924, also created a shortage of manpower for the sugar plantations of the neighboring Island of Saint Croix. Thousands of Puerto Ricans were recruited for these jobs. Today Puerto Ricans make up one of the most numerous and influential groups on the island of Saint Croix. The pioneer study by Dr. Clarence Senior on Puerto Rican emigration to Saint Croix sheds considerable light on this emigratory exodus.[15]

In one of his most recent books, Dr. Gordon K. Lewis has pointed out the following with respect to the emigration of Puerto Ricans to Saint Croix:

> A conservative estimate of the incidence of first-generation Virgin Islanders who are of Puerto Rican descent would be around 25 percent, with the figure significantly higher for St. Croix, alone. . . . the demographic pattern of the Puerto Ricans indicates a fairly widespread penetration in both urban and rural areas. The original wave emerged from the decaying economies of the Puerto Rican islets of Vieques and Culebra, and the number of immigrants increased significantly after 1927, when U.S. immigration legislation was applied to the Virgin Islands. Whereas in the first generation there was a heavy percentage of field workers among the new migrants, who replaced Crucian workers deserting the land because of the equation of rural work with low social status, the second generation has moved into a more heterogeneous employment pattern.[16]

This Puerto Rican presence in Saint Croix has served Dr. Sydney Mintz as a basis for comparing the conditions of the emigrants to Hawaii and those who settled in Saint Croix.[17] We are not interested in that polemic because we consider it sterile. We *are* interested, of course, in the different experiences of Puerto Rican emigrants in their most diverse contexts, without stopping to determine which of the emigrant groups best assimilated the capitalist ethic.

Let us proceed now to the decade of the 1930s. As will be recalled, this is the decade of the Great Capitalist Depression, a period, in many ways, similar to that in which we are presently living. The first thing to note is that the depression not only stopped the emigratory process during that decade, but that it also produced—as it is producing right now—a movement in which those who had emigrated were returning to the Island. Chenault points out accordingly that "During the worst years of the depression, there was a net movement back to Puerto Rico. Beginning in the year 1934, there is again an excess of immigration to the United States."[18]

According to the statistics provided by the Centro de Estudios Demográficos (Center for Demographic Studies) of the University of Puerto Rico, some 90,000 Puerto Ricans emigrated to the United States from the moment of the U.S. occupation until 1944, an average of 2,000 emigrants per year during that period of time. When this figure is contrasted to those of the net emigration of Puerto Ricans beginning with the end of World War II, it will be noted that we are not exaggerating when we speak of a mass exodus of Puerto Ricans.

The brief retrospective look that we have tried to offer in this chapter is certainly fragmentary and incomplete. More thorough and conscientious studies are needed on all these episodes of our national history. We believe, nevertheless, that the socio-historic focus of these events is peremptory, and urgent for my people.

Those who have had to emigrate during this century have offered a burning testimony, for the present and future generations of our people, of the phenomenon of exploitation, exile and the insensitivity of those who consciously propitiate this emigratory exodus. The history of our people is also the history of those who had to leave. To omit this reality in any historic account of our people not only perverts the analysis, but constitutes an act of crass historic irresponsibility.

*As a nation founded on what there is that is
human on earth, it seems so insecure,
dazzling only to the nearsighted, where after
three centuries of democracy, with one tilt of
the law, it can happen that the government
is asked now to take upon its shoulders the
life of the poor masses. Where the sum total
of selfishness, driven mad by the pleasure of
triumph or the fear of misery, creates,
instead of a people of one firm weave, a
doughy mass of individuals without support,
who divide among themselves and flee as
soon as they no longer feel the pull of the
community of mutual benefits. Where all the
problems of hate from the old human
continent have been transferred here,
without that intimate and soothing
communion with the soil.*

JOSÉ MARTÍ

4

THE GREAT METROPOLIS

According to the census of the United States, in 1974 the Puerto Rican
population residing in the United States climbed to a total of 1.5 million
people, at least one million of whom, it is conservatively estimated,
lived in New York City.[1] However, this total has been disputed not only
by a recent study of the Puerto Rican Socialist Party (Partido Socialista
Puertorriqueño, PSP)—which concludes that there are two million
Puerto Ricans living in the United States, of whom 1,250,000 reside in
New York—but also by a study of the United States Commission on
Civil Rights.[2] It seems to us that the number of Puerto Ricans residing
in the United States—especially in New York City—is greater than the
total indicated by the federal census. In any case, it is necessary to take
into full consideration the magnitude of the problem: more Puerto
Ricans reside in New York City alone than in San Juan, the capital of
Puerto Rico.

To what do we attribute the controversy over the exact number of

Puerto Ricans who reside in New York City or in the rest of the United States? The question revolves around the problem of who is or is not Puerto Rican. On the island of Puerto Rico, the question does not seem to constitute a very complex problem: Puerto Ricans are all those who have been born in Puerto Rico, or who, having been born outside of the Island, are children of Puerto Rican parents. It should be noted that here the Puerto Rican is defined by purely geographic (born on the Island) or genealogical (Puerto Rican parentage) criteria. According to this definition, it matters little whether or not the person identifies with the fundamental characteristics of Puerto Rican national culture. That is reason enough for it to be preferable, perhaps, to say that the person who meets the criteria mentioned above is *potentially* a Puerto Rican, leaving to be determined in the future whether or not this person is to be integrated into the cultural currents that define Puerto Rico as a society belonging to the Latin American cultural family. In fact, the geographic and genealogical criteria mentioned above, granting that they are important, are nevertheless less important than the cultural criteria with respect to the definition of a nationality. From this perspective, not all those born in Puerto Rico or of Puerto Rican parents are Puerto Ricans when seen in light of their integration into the Puerto Rican national culture. We maintain, therefore, that the determining factor of whether or not a person is Puerto Rican lies in the cultural question as the definitive central element of his or her Puerto Ricanness.

Puerto Rico is a society with a national culture and it has therefore its own profile and definition, even when it is found to be subjected to a systematic process of cultural penetration and dissolution, which in another context we have called "The Siege of Puerto Rican Culture." In spite of this fact, the vast majority of those who reside on the Island identify themselves as Puerto Ricans when asked about their nationality. We do not want to brush aside the serious problem of the Puerto Rican's identity. We have first-hand knowledge of the cultural schizophrenia from which we suffer as a result of the ambivalent and subordinating relationship to which colonialism condemns us. In spite of that fact, however, there exists a cultural sediment, a basic substratum of experiences, habits, customs, language, etc., that define us as a people.

Let us look at the Puerto Rican community in the United States. The first thing to note here is an undeniable social fact: the Puerto Ricans who live in the United States live outside of the Puerto Rican national territory. They find themselves transplanted from their native country to another territory whose land does not belong to them, and is foreign to them (legally and existentially speaking). This is only insofar as geography is concerned. But the question cannot be limited to this aspect. Let us take things from a generational perspective. We have seen how the heaviest emigration to the United States takes place in the period immediately following World War II. Before this exodus there were only some 60,000 *Boricuas* in New York. Those people had emigrated for the most part before World War II.

Today, we can distinguish between various generations of Puerto Ricans in the United States. First of all, there are those who emigrated before 1940. These are people who are now elderly and who, when they arrived in the United States, were already formed culturally. Then we have the emigrants of the postwar period who, generally speaking, are today middle-aged people whose children are born in the United States. And lastly, we have those Puerto Ricans born in the United States, beginning approximately in 1950, whose parents are Puerto Rican. These younger people are already the parents of a new generation of Puerto Rican children who not only were born outside of the Island but have in general a very limited knowledge of the Island.

Let us concentrate on the first Puerto Rican generation born in New York after the mass emigration of the 1950s. The United States census classifies them as "of Puerto Rican origin" when one of their parents is of Puerto Rican origin. These youths have been born in, and have become part of the social fabric of the United States. Their parents are from Puerto Rico, speak Spanish among themselves, and maintain cultural and personal ties with the Island. Nevertheless, an important difference exists between a youth of Puerto Rican origin born in New York and one born in Puerto Rico. The former is born in a country where Puerto Rican nationality is found to be a minority nationality, where the vernacular language is English, and where one's vital experiences take place within the framework of U.S. culture. The latter, on the other hand, is born in a society with definite geographical contours, where the vernacular is Spanish and where the cultural context remains defined within the framework of Puerto Rican society. We repeat: the United States census defines "Puerto Rican" in purely genealogical, and to a lesser degree, geographic terms, whereas in Puerto Rico, we define it in cultural and social terms. The cultural question does not interest the metropolis because it is a matter of one more ethnic

minority within U.S. society. For the metropolis, it is simply a matter of
"Americans of Puerto Rican origin," or "Puerto Rican Americans."
For us, however, what defines the Puerto Rican is fundamentally the
cultural question, a contention that we will discuss more extensively in
another chapter of this book. More than twice the number of Puerto
Ricans live in New York City than in San Juan, the capital of Puerto
Rico. In one borough alone of New York City—the Bronx—there is a
Puerto Rican population that numerically exceeds that of many of the
principal cities of the Island. There are also small towns bordering New
York City with Puerto Rican communities which have been practically
transplanted from the rural regions of Puerto Rico. In this sense,
Puerto Ricans are found dispersed among many of the principal cities
of the Eastern United States, and also with considerable concentrations
in some cities on the Pacific Coast.[3]

New York City, that "great urban center," is what serves as
magnetic pole for most Puerto Ricans. Puerto Ricans constitute ten
percent of the city's residents. They make up the lowest rung of the
social ladder, the most alienated from the power structures of the
metropolis, among those who suffer with greatest intensity the process
of exploitation suffered also by Afro-Americans, Native Americans,
Chicanos, Asian-Americans, West Indians, Dominicans, etc. Crowded
into the dilapidated tenements of the South Bronx or Spanish Harlem
("El Barrio"), forced to live under subhuman conditions in Manhattan's Lower East Side, our people are pushed with greater intensity
every day toward pauperism, dependency, and collective impotence.[4]
These are not mere rhetorical phrases, but rather the bare reality that
confronts the vast majority of *Boricuas* in the "great urban center."

Some general statistics might contribute to clear up the question.
The same source quoted above—the United States census for 1974—
indicates that of all the Spanish-speaking residents in the United States,
Puerto Ricans are those with the lowest incomes. The 1975 *Current
Population Survey* confirms this once again.[5] The average Puerto
Rican income, for example, is $7,629 per family, in comparison to that
of Chicanos ($9,498) and other minority groups ($11,500). Compare
this to the average income of U.S. families ($12,836) and we see that the
income of Puerto Rican families is only slightly more than half of the
income of U.S. families. From this point of view, the situation in 1974 is
not very different from what it was in 1970, when a study carried out in
New York City showed that 32.6 percent of Puerto Ricans were found

to be living below the poverty level.[6] This study also documents the difficult access of Puerto Ricans to education. For example, the average education for Puerto Ricans was eight and one-half years in 1970. For that same year, one out of every five Puerto Ricans over twenty-five had a high school diploma, while only one out of every hundred Puerto Ricans over twenty-five had a college diploma. It goes without saying that the access of our people to graduate and post-graduate education is even more limited than what we have indicated here.

Given these circumstances, it should not surprise us if *Boricuas* confirm the infamous and racist "self-fulfilling prophecy," that they do not progress because they lack education and that they lack education because they do not progress.

Let us take an additional index. We saw earlier that one of the characteristics of capitalist development is the hurling of thousands and thousands of people into the orbit of pauperism. That tendency is manifested among Puerto Ricans residing in the metropolis, especially in New York City. In a study done by Nicholas Kinsburg, consultant to New York Councilman Andrew J. Stein, it was found that approximately half of the Puerto Ricans residing in New York City were on welfare.[7] This fact is often taken as an index of the indolence and idleness of our people, when the truth is that the exploitation they suffer at the hands of bosses, landlords, bureaucrats, etc. forces the immense majority of them to swell the state welfare lists. Here, also, racial prejudice against the Puerto Rican community is unleashed, while the media babbles nonsense about the "parasitism" of our compatriots.

As if all this were not enough, a study done by Drs. Joseph P. Fitzpatrick and Robert E. Gould showed that the percentage of mental illnesses among Puerto Rican residents in New York City was "abnormally high," tripling the incidence of common mental illnesses in the rest of the population. For example, it was found that 102.5 of every 100,000 Puerto Ricans suffered from mental illnesses in contrast to 34.5 per 100,000 for the entire state of New York. Among the causes of these illnesses, the researchers mention "stress from migration, including uprooting, adjustment to a new way of life. . . ."[8] But it is clear that this high incidence of mental illnesses is the product of intolerable situations created by the clash and conflict with a society that disowns and scorns us. It is worth the effort to stress the poisonous effects of extreme poverty and pauperism on these mental syndromes. It is not, therefore, due to the "mercurial" nature of *Boricuas,* nor because we are "tropical" and other such nonsense that we suffer to a greater degree from mental illnesses, but rather because of the alienating and inhuman character of the society, in which the structures created by imperialism press us down.

A larger number of Puerto Ricans is concentrated in the "great urban center" of New York City than in the capital of Puerto Rico itself. But as we have already seen, under terrible conditions. Our objective is not to evoke a Dantesque hell, but rather to describe with utmost precision the condition of Puerto Ricans in New York City. We could expand our discussion by using statistics on drug addiction, crime and juvenile delinquency among our people in New York. We could also offer the reader the other side of the coin: the Puerto Ricans who have "progressed," those who live in the suburbs of New York City or who are included among those who boast of being millionaires. The former cannot be understood without the latter, which is why it is imperative that we enter into the following considerations.

One of the characteristics of the ethics of capitalism is its insistence that social mobility is an individual action, perfectly attainable for all those willing to work hard and be frugal. Upward social mobility is, therefore, "proof" that a person has been able to overcome his or her limitations produced by impoverished living conditions, and has joined the company of those who had previously looked down on him or her. This ethic of capitalism, described with singular brilliance by Marx and Weber, has always been the ideology, the convenient reinforcement for the ruling class in its effort to incorporate—and therefore neutralize— the most prominent among the exploited classes, managing in this way to revive and sustain the myth of "equal opportunity." Those who succeed in "arriving" at certain posts or positions are immediately cele- brated by the mass media which is at the service of the system.

It was merely a question of time before assimilation of emigrants of European origin would take place through the process which Glazer and Moynihan call nearing "the Anglo-Saxon center."[9] But when it came to "incorporating" Afro-Americans, Chicanos, Asians and Puer- to Ricans, the tune has been a different one. In a society which is racist to the marrow, the groups classified as non-whites have to pay a higher, more costly price than that which emigrants of European descent had to pay when they took up the road of assimilation into U.S. society.

The Civil Rights Movement of the 1960s used the now familiar term "tokenism" in order to describe the practice of incorporating a single Black into the United States Supreme Court, or into a school for whites in Alabama, or some office previously all white, etc. in Boston. But "tokenism" is a racist ideological weapon, presented to us as "proof" that the system is open to talent and ability, that any Black youth who makes the effort and studies eagerly can capture the peak scaled by, for example, Judge Thurgood Marshall.

We Puerto Ricans fall precisely within that classification of non-whites, an objective definition which the system itself has given us and which has nothing to do with the desires of some Puerto Ricans to have it changed. And this is so not only because our population is in fact racially mixed, but because according to U.S. criteria, anyone who lives south of the Rio Grande in one way or another belongs to an inferior race. We Puerto Ricans are far from constituting an exception to that rule.

The fundamental racist character of U.S. capitalist society cements and reinforces prejudice against our people. The educational level or the economic advancement of some Puerto Ricans "chosen" as models of triumph against adversity matters little. These "chosen few" note immediately that they cannot escape the stereotypes deeply rooted in the U.S. monopoly-dominated environment. For example, a so-called form of "praising" a *Boricua* in the "great urban center" is by means of the phrase, hurled like a dart: "You don't look Puerto Rican." Of course, the fact that you might not "look Puerto Rican" is also a reflection of the virtues of a civilization that rejects us. To not look Puerto Rican becomes a categorical imperative of the racist system which associates "inferior" races with the most servile tasks within the social register.

In order for the Puerto Rican to "not look Puerto Rican," he or she has to adopt the norms and values of the society that denies his or her identity. For example, we have Mr. Manuel Casiano Junior (Manny), whose accomplishments in the banking field have led him to amass a huge fortune. This *Boricuan* version of Horatio Alger has become one of the most fervent advertisers of the "American Way of Life." The system is open to anyone who will work hard and learn the rules of the game: so "Manny" Casiano seems to say, from his luxurious ten-room apartment on Park Avenue.

Also present on the New York scene is ex-Congressman from the Bronx and former Deputy Mayor of New York City, Attorney Herman

Badillo. Hailing from the city of Caguas, Puerto Rico, Mr. Badillo was admitted to the bar in New York, culminating his political career with his election to the United States Congress. Badillo is a skilled person in the political machinery of New York City, having managed to bring about, at least up until now, an alliance between impoverished Puerto Ricans and a Jewish middle class, who gave him their votes for a seat in Washington representing the South Bronx.

It is no accident that both Badillo and Casiano have been presented to us as archetypes of the Puerto Rican community by *New York Magazine.* The issue in question is extremely interesting, in that it shows how many North Americans—including in this case the liberals—perceive us. Here, for example, is an excerpt from this magazine which presents the ruling class view in clearly racist tones.

Let us listen:

These people were "Spanish." They came in swarms like ants turning the sidewalks brown, and they settled in, multiplied, whole sections of the city fallen to their shiny black raincoats and chewing-gum speech. We called them "mee-dahs," because they were always shouting "mee-dah, mee-dah,"* with a presumptuous sense of wonder. Look at what? The subway, the sky, the Long Island Sound turned the color of dark rum by the sheer congestion of their bodies?

I did not hate them or fear them or even feel disgusted by them. I only knew they grew in numbers rather than stature, that they were neither white nor black but some indelicate tan, and that they were here, irrevocably; the best you could do to avoid contamination was to keep them out of mind. And if they got too close—well, the smell of beans and beer, whole families eating chicken, gnawing down to the bone, pink walls and cockamamie music, endless bongos in the night—well, there would be this greaser with hair like an oily palm tree, and he'd be sitting next to you in the subway in his Desi Arnaz shoes and his silver sharkskin pants and his jukebox-bolero-shirt, and you just knew he had a razor up his sleeve. And his old lady with the Bueno Bargains ballgown and the breasts that spread like Staten Island: where were they going anyway, the two of them, at a time when all the decent people were either working the night shift or sitting home watching *Your Hit Parade?*

We lived in the Projects, where everyone aspired to be above himself. Our Spanish neighbors spoke English to us, and they weren't on welfare. Still, I found myself wondering:

Do they have a parrot?

*"Mira" ("Look") in Spanish.

> How can they fry bananas?
>
> What was life like in the jungle?
>
> Where do they sharpen their shoes?
>
> I never ventured to inquire. It was enough to know I was above them; that gave me a sense of *noblesse oblige,* so that I was quite friendly, as most WASPS are to me: aliens are to be appreciated for their "ethnic diversity." Or put another way: the lower classes got nice asses.[10]

Of course, after the racist insults, they have to present the brighter side of the picture. And that is where "Manny" Casiano and Herman Badillo come in. Puerto Rican young people of "El Barrio" and the South Bronx should not be discouraged, because if they apply themselves and work hard they can become millionaires like Casiano or congressmen like Badillo. The problem lies, nevertheless, in the fact that the living conditions for the vast majority of Puerto Ricans in New York are such that the chances of their even being able to get out of the ghetto are extremely remote. There exists, admittedly, a sector of middle-class Puerto Ricans who have migrated to the suburbs of New York City. But their numerical importance is clearly clouded over by a Puerto Rican population which is eminently proletarian.

This is even more true when we compare the economic-social condition of Puerto Ricans residing in New York during three different historic periods. Let us take first the situation in the 1930s, when—according to the first important sociological study on emigration to New York, that of Professor Lawrence Chenault—we are offered the following picture of *Boricuas* in New York:

> The social adjustment necessitated by the migration results from the abrupt change of people but slightly removed from the peasant class from a simple rural environment to the slum section of an enormous city. The migration causes disintegrating forces to affect the family. In addition to this painful adjustment, the worker and his family are exposed to conditions which have long been recognized as harmful to the happiness and well-being of all people regardless of background. Often mixed with other families under extremely crowded conditions, without funds or employment, and in many cases suffering from malnutrition or some chronic disease, it is not strange that the worker and his family feel the influence of the antisocial behavior which is prevalent in these neighborhoods. Having come from an island where he has already acquired a feeling of mistreatment at the hands of the American people and their government, he [the Puerto Rican worker] is often resentful as a result of the clash in culture, racial antagonisms, and the failure to realize many expectations because of what he feels are discrimination and indifference.[11]

It is worth the effort to observe that the total Puerto Rican population at that historic moment did not exceed 50,000 people, and that Professor Chenault considers us a relatively small Hispanic contingent. It is important to observe, moreover, that because that was the decade of the depression, the flow and ebb of emigration is considerable. We observe in the 1930s a tendency of many Puerto Ricans to return to the Island as a result of the adverse economic conditions found in the metropolis. In the book just cited, we also find documentation of the serious problems of cultural adjustment suffered by Puerto Ricans, the eminently proletarian character of the majority of the emigrants, the fact that the majority of these workers are unskilled, etc. In summary, Puerto Rican emigrants residing in New York during the 1930s lived under conditions of extreme poverty and dehumanization.

A little more than ten years later, a group of social science researchers from Columbia University, led by the great sociologist C. Wright Mills, did a study on Puerto Rican emigrants in New York City. Note that we are now dealing with the postwar period and that the study is done precisely when the Law of Industrial Incentives (1947)—"Fomento" in Puerto Rico—is passed. Let us listen to the descriptions by Mills and his colleagues of the Puerto Rican migrant:

> Occupational mobility of the Puerto Ricans in New York is quite restricted: they are concentrated in lower skilled jobs, and their chances to rise above them seem rather slim. In the journey to New York, most of the migrants do not experience a rise in the level of their job, many in fact are now at lower levels than they held in Puerto Rico. For some, this downward mobility is a new experience, for others it is a continuation of a downward mobility already experienced on the island from the occupational position of their fathers. Still others, who have risen in jobs in coming to New York, have only regained the job status once held by their fathers . . .

> As successive waves of immigrants have swept into Manhattan and elsewhere in America, a rather clear-cut pattern of their experience and of the reactions of native Americans has been established. Most of the newcomers are poor, and hence forced into the least desirable sections of the city, from two to ten families often living in accommodations built for one. They are uneducated; the ways of the new city are strange and complex; the ways of yet another culture add to their strangeness and complexity; they are exploited by native landlords and sharks, and by some of their own countrymen who already "know the ropes." Entering the labor market, unlearned, unskilled, they seem at the mercy of economic forces. If the business cycle is on the upturn, they are welcome; if it is on the way down, or in the middle of one of its periodic breakdowns, there is a savage struggle for even the low wage jobs between the new immigrants and the earlier ones who feel they have a prior claim.[12]

It is worthwhile to emphasize the phenomenon of "downward mobility" or descending mobility. The mythology of capitalism looks—in accordance with what we have already observed—to create in the exploited classes the feeling that social ascension is not really denied them. Nevertheless, the hard facts impose themselves over these pious myths.

Let us come closer to our present time. In 1970, a study done with all the methodology and categories of the positivist focus, was to inform us of the following: "Only 16.7 percent of the migrants are in white collar occupations, as compared with 32.9 percent of the Island inhabitants and 44.0 percent of the return migrants."[13] Another even more recent study, that of Kal Wagenheim, reinforces this thesis. The conclusions of this study—based on figures from the United States census—with respect to the level of incomes, education and unemployment, are the following:

a. *income level.* In 1970, the federal government defined poverty as an income of $3,740 or less for a family of four, or $4,415 for a family of five. That year, 283,000 Puerto Rican New Yorkers were in poverty, and an additional. . . . 30,000 Puerto Ricans were in the near-poor category, with incomes only 25 percent above the poverty definition. This means that . . . 45 percent of the Puerto Ricans in the city were either poor or near-poor.[14]

b. *education* . . . Puerto Ricans . . . constitute 22.8 percent of the city's classroom enrollment. The city had only 978 Puerto Rican teachers—only 1.1 percent of the teaching staff.[15]

c. *unemployment.* According to March, 1972 figures, Puerto Ricans have the highest unemployment rate of virtually all ethnic or racial groups in the United States. While 6 percent of all U.S. men were jobless, the figure was 7.4 percent for men of Spanish origin, and 8.8 percent for Puerto Rican men. Among women, unemployment was 6.6 percent nationwide, 10 percent for women of Spanish origin, and 17.6 percent for Puerto Rican women.

These figures do not describe the true picture. It is worse. The rate of unemployment refers to that portion of the civilian labor force that is jobless. However, the "civilian labor force" is not synonymous with the entire working-age population. It includes only those persons who are working or actively seeking work. It does not include disabled persons. It does not include persons who, for various reasons (lack of skills, lack of opportunity in geographic area, and so forth) are not actively seeking work. In other words, the chronically unemployed, those who have lost hope, are not included in official unemployment statistics.

For example, 86 percent of all Americans, ages 16 to 64, are in the labor force. Among Puerto Ricans, the figure drops to 76.6 percent. If Puerto

Ricans participated in the labor force at the same level as the total population and the number of persons with jobs remained constant, unemployment among Puerto Rican men would be more accurately depicted—not at the "official" rate of 8.8 percent—but at the "adjusted" (and more realistic) level of 18.7 percent. Among Puerto Rican women, the "official" rate of 17.6 percent "adjusts" upward to 56.4 percent. For both men and women, the "official" rate of 12.6 percent soars to 33.0 percent.[16]

We are quoting from these studies somewhat extensively because we consider it essential that these incontestable statistics be known. Moreover, we want to establish that this happens within the city whose standard of living is higher than that of most of the cities of the world. The social inequality as it related to Puerto Ricans has not changed during the last thirty or forty years, in fact, it has been intensified. Reformist panaceas have simply intensified pauperism with all its resulting evils.

According to the U.S. census projections, the Puerto Rican population in the United States and on the Island will eventually match up. Within this context, the mammoth Puerto Rican population in New York City takes on a singular importance, since New York is a kind of giant mirror where all Puerto Ricans can look at ourselves. In that "great urban center," the problems of the Puerto Rican community stand out because of their very magnitude and profundity. We could say that New York City is a kind of giant mural where all the vicissitudes of our people are represented within an urban and highly industrialized setting.

Moreover, New York City itself is changing its face very rapidly. Besides the serious economic crisis that the city is facing at the present moment, we are observing—again as cause and effect of the same reality—an exodus of the most important manufacturing companies to the outskirts of the city, and a great population exodus of whites to the suburban areas of the city.

With respect to this exodus of businesses, *Fortune* magazine reported that 25 percent of the largest companies established in New York City had decided to move. A report on this very point indicates:

> A number of companies had moved to the area where many key employees—particularly the chief executives—live. Other considerations that are rarely mentioned, but sometimes considered when a move is made ... are the number of blacks and Puerto Ricans in the city, crime against persons and property and a dislike of the physical environments.[17]

Still more, there exists such a pronounced tendency to abandon

the main area of New York City, that according to a private organization studying this problem, it is conjectured that the city will be left
"primarily with unemployed and the retired poor."[18] This would un-
doubtedly lead to the even greater displacement of the Puerto Rican
work force in the city. New York is rapidly turning into a city which
provides services. This tendency can only intensify the severity of the
problem of Puerto Rican unemployment, especially if we keep in mind
that our work force is principally unskilled or semi-skilled.

The enormous concentration of Puerto Ricans in New York City
allows us to know firsthand the disastrous effects of a mass exodus
which has placed them right in the neurological center of the great
capitalist metropolis. In the "great urban center," all the sores of
capitalism become more visible and throbbing. For the Puerto Ricans
who live under subhuman conditions in the South Bronx, or on the
Lower East Side, the "American Way of Life," more than being a
propagandist slogan, constitutes a grotesque mockery in the face of
their condition of pauperism. Prisoners of the ghetto, victims of
harassment and racial prejudice, deprived of the most basic tools for
their struggle for human dignity, the Puerto Ricans who live in New
York daily resist the designs of the system to dehumanize them. But
even more important is the fact that, unlike their compatriots on the
Island, Puerto Ricans in "New York exile" come to know first-hand
and directly what U.S. capitalist society really is. This knowledge gives
them extraordinary revolutionary potential for the struggle for Puerto
Rican liberation. The Puerto Ricans residing in New York have the
potential and capacity to carry the revolutionary struggle to the very
heart of the oppressor society. Just as the Algerians did in their day, or
as the Irish have been doing for years, the *Boricuas* can be a battering
ram capable of pounding away at the empire in its most vulnerable
points.

In addition to this, the Puerto Rican proletariat of New York City
can and should participate together with other ethnic groups who suffer
exploitation (Blacks, Chicanos, Asian Americans, etc.) as well as with
the most progressive sectors within the U.S. working class in a frontal
attack on capitalism and on behalf of socialism. The one is not
incompatible with the other. On the contrary. these are complementary
actions.

Up until today, Puerto Rican emigrants in New York have suc-
cessfully resisted all attempts directed toward the destruction of their

national profiles. Just as on the Island, the Puerto Rican working class in the metropolis ought to play a dominant role in the struggle for national liberation and socialism. It is an internationalist struggle, but it should not, however, lose sight—as Lenin constantly warned us—of the fact that the weakening of imperialism through the successful struggle of national liberation movements is a categorical imperative for all revolutionaries. The support and solidarity for the national liberation struggle and the struggle for socialism in the metropolis are complementary, not conflicting strategies. To say that they are in conflict would be to deny the essential significance of the struggle for the liberation of our people.

> *As soon as capitalist production takes
> possession of agriculture, and in proportion
> to the extent to which it does so, the
> demand for an agricultural labouring
> population falls absolutely, while the
> accumulation of the capital employed in
> agriculture advances, without this repulsion
> being, as in non-agricultural industries,
> compensated by a greater attraction.*
>
> KARL MARX

5

THE AGRICULTURAL EMIGRANTS

In an excellent article on agricultural emigrants, Professor Ricardo Puerta has written:

> In 1970, around 50,000 Puerto Ricans left the Island to labor as agricultural peons for eight months or less in the farms located in the United States. These workers for the most part go to work in the fields of the northeast region of the North American nation, but principally in the states of Connecticut, Delaware, Massachusetts, New Jersey, New York, Ohio and Pennsylvania. Upon finishing their seasonal work they return to Puerto Rico where they spend the rest of the year, and perhaps repeat the migratory experience the following year.[1]

Although the conditions of the Puerto Rican emigrants located in the large U.S. metropolises are, as we have demonstrated, conditions of abject poverty, they are in any case much better than those conditions that serve as a kind of daily burden for *Boricuan* agricultural workers. From the studies done on the condition of the agricultural emigrants, there emerges the bleak picture of exploitation, misery, horrible working conditions and especially crass irresponsibility on the part of the Puerto Rican colonial authorities charged by law to watch over and assure the rights of these compatriots. However, this has not prevented an entire Commission of Labor of the Puerto Rican House of Representatives from painting a rather rosy picture of life in the agricultural fields of the U.S. where thousands of Puerto Ricans toil. This Commission, after a short visit to the agricultural camps in the northeast of the

United States, concluded that "there is no discrimination in the North nor in the South against *Boricuan* workers," limiting itself to recommend, among other things, "that the phrase 'agricultural worker' be substituted for 'migrant worker,' since the word 'migrant' in itself carries with it a kind of humiliation and could wound the dignity of these compatriots."[2] As if the problem could be remedied through mere semantic exercises!

Once again we must combat the purely psychological condition of the emigratory phenomenon. We have in the east of the United States a whole group of corporations dedicated to capitalist agricultural exploitation. Some of these corporations are tied to great transnational corporations, like Gulf and Western. In Puerto Rico we have, on the other hand, an agriculture which has been on the decline since the postwar period (1947) and an excessive emphasis on industrialization as the panacea for our enduring evils. Given those circumstances, one can explain the reason for the exodus of agricultural workers to the farms producing tobacco, asparagus, tomatoes, etc. in the United States. We have in this case two economic factors of vital importance: on the one hand there is a large contingent of agricultural workers displaced by the structural transformations of the Puerto Rican economy, and the simple numerical proportion of these workers lowers the salaries offered them by the U.S. agricultural companies. To this factor must be added the competition of agricultural workers from the West Indies and other countries of the Caribbean. Moreover, the present capitalist economic crisis has sharpened the problem of unemployment in the metropolis itself, which is why many U.S. workers who previously refused to work in agriculture, today accept jobs of this kind in the very communities in which they live.

In the second place, the Puerto Rican agricultural workers offer the U.S. agricultural enterprises not only an abundant work force, but a cheap one. This is the product, first, of the fact that agricultural workers are not covered by the U.S. government's minimum wage laws, and, second, of the fact that these workers lack the power derived from unionization. This last factor, in spite of the extraordinary effort by a group of workers who have founded the Asociación de Trabajadores Agrícolas (ATA, The Association of Agricultural Workers) and who are waging a great struggle on behalf of emigrant agricultural workers, greatly favors the agricultural corporations. These corporate exploiters use the "excess population" as a labor reserve which is attracted or repelled by the system according to the system's needs.

The agricultural worker is displaced by the transition from a social formation based on agriculture to one based on the process of industrialization. Nevertheless, we would be mistaken if we saw this displacement as one based on transformations of a purely technological nature. We are dealing with something even more profound. All these structural transformations of the Puerto Rican economy are products of the needs and demands of the economy of the capitalist metropolis of the world, and our people, in the main, have been passive spectators in that whole process. In a capitalist-colonial economy they could not take those necessary measures so that those who were suffering more severely the changes of the new economic orientation could readapt themselves to the new social situation. This is particularly true of the agricultural workers. Very much to the contrary, the Puerto Rican colonial authorities concentrated all their efforts, beginning in 1947, to promote emigration as the principal solution to the problem—for them unsolvable by other means—of overpopulation.

Throughout this book we have repeatedly emphasized a fundamental question: that Puerto Rican emigration has been encouraged and promoted by the government of the "Free Associated State" of Puerto Rico, in spite of the protests of their leaders that they "neither stimulate nor discourage emigration." Nevertheless, the evidence to the contrary is extremely convincing. As a matter of fact, there has been a complete orientation of public activity directed toward the promotion of emigration. Both in the content and form of this orientation, the alleged *necessity* of "emigration" as an "escape valve" for the "population problems" of the Island has been absorbing the thinking of the colonial political leaders. Beginning in 1947, with the establishment of the Program of "Fomento Económico," we see with greater clarity "the tonic" that is to guide the theory and practice of the Puerto Rican colonial elite from that historic moment on. An example is the following recommendation of the Planning Board of the Governor of Puerto Rico—led at that time by Dr. Rafael Picó—referring to Puerto Rican emigration.

Relatively few Puerto Rican women have come to the Continental United States during the postwar migratory movements. Recently, however, the Insular Governor has been studying plans for the emigration of Puerto Ricans to the Continental United States and other countries. One proposal is for the emigration of Puerto Rican women to the United States to provide domestic services. It has been expressed that the emigration of women not only alleviates the present condition of unemployment, but also assures its beneficial effects in the long run by helping to reduce birth control.[3]

These recommendations should be seen in conjunction with the creation of an "Advisory Committee on Emigration" (Comité Asesor Sobre la Emigración) which met in the Executive Mansion during 1947 and 1948. This committee, among whose members were such government leaders as Luis Muñoz Marín, Teodoro Moscoso, Rafael Pico, Vicente Geigel Polanco, Fernando Sierra Berdecía, Ramón Colón Torres, as well as such ideologues of emigration as Clarence Senior and Paul Hatt, discussed seriously and thoroughly the possibility and desirability of "relocating" (this is the euphemism) Puerto Ricans in other American and European countries. It sould be noted that in the minutes of a meeting held in the residence of Dr. Rafael Pico on July 29, 1947—a copy of which has been made available to us by Attorney Salvador Tío, Jr., Director of the Migrant Program of the Office of Legal Services of Puerto Rico—the following objectives are made explicit: a) to stabilize the population of Puerto Rico at its present level; b) to achieve a reduction of 25 percent in order to stabilize the population at around 1,500,000 inhabitants. It then goes on to affirm the following:

> To reach the first objective, it would be necessary to set up a program for the emigration of 50,000 people per year for an indefinite period. To reach the second, it would be necessary to set up a program for the emigration of 100,000 per year for ten years . . . The total emigration for these first ten years would be 1,000,000 inhabitants. This figure breaks down into the 500,000 people we have to subtract from the present population plus the 500,000 who would represent the natural increase in the population. From then on, the emigration program should be limited to 50,000 per year, until those changes that have been responsible for the population stabilization in other countries are well in operation.

It is imperative to point out two things: 1) that the objective of the discussion at this stage was directed toward the emigration of Puerto Ricans to Latin America, preferably to Brazil and Venezuela; and 2) that those who were discussing these alternatives were officials of the highest administrative levels who submitted their recommendations in writing to the Secretary of Labor of Puerto Rico. In like manner, we can deduce from reading the minutes of these high-level meetings that the emigration question stemmed from the assumption that there exists "a disbalance between the population and the natural resources of

Puerto Rico," and therefore to no one's surprise, emigration has been advanced as one of the principle strategies for resolving the economic problems of Puerto Rico.

Even more, the authors appear to be worried by the effects of what they call "The Puerto Rican Problem" in New York City, especially if a recession in the metropolis were to create an excess labor force that the system could not absorb. In such a case, they tell us, it would be necessary to seek other areas for the relocation of the emigrants, thus opening up the possibility of emigration to South America, especially Brazil.

Remember, it is on May 9, 1947 that Law 87 passes, and we hear, underscored over and over again: "The Governor of Puerto Rico neither stimulates nor promotes the emigration of Puerto Rican workers to the United States or to any foreign country." And in that very same year, the elaborate "rationale" for the mass exodus of Puerto Ricans, which we have already witnessed, was being schemed in La Fortaleza. We are dealing, of course, with two levels of political work. First, the work which is going to serve as the basis for public consumption (Law 89 in 1947, or the subsequent law passed by the Puerto Rican Legislative Assembly on June 22, 1962), which pretends a government hands-off policy with respect to emigration. Second, there is the historic and very concrete fact that this emigration was being discussed in the highest government circles which were fully aware of its consequences and which were against a presumptive legislation that would have contradicted those objectives. In time the position of the high officials of the Executive Branch prevailed, especially that of the technocrats who would wind up dominating the political orientation of the Partido Popular Democrático (PPD, Popular Democratic Party), beginning with the end of World War II.

We are dealing with two phases of the same reality. The promotion of Puerto Rican emigration continues to be an indisputable fact today. According to Law 87 of 1947, the Governor of Puerto Rico neither promotes nor stimulates emigration. But eight years later, the president of the Planning Board of the "Free Associated State," Mr. Cándido Oliveras, could send the following "candid" report to the Provisional Governor of Puerto Rico at that time (1955), *don* Roberto Sánchez Vilella, about the perspectives of Puerto Rican emigration:

Unless the net external movement of the population exceeds 60,000 per year, the *labor* force will grow rapidly and an increase in unemployment is

expected. In view of the probability of the continued increase in unemployment, the policies and decisions that directly or indirectly affect the external
movement of the population ought to favor this movement. Provided that
this is possible and consistent with political considerations, the decisions,
programs and policies that promote the external movement ought to be
carried out. Due to the rapid growth of the labor force during the next six or
seven years, even the revenue anticipated at the level of economic activity
will be insufficient for maintaining unemployment at the present levels
unless the population movement to the outside exceeds 60,000 per year.[4]

Thus, there is no room for any doubt regarding the political
orientation of the Governor of Puerto Rico as far as emigration was
concerned. We are dealing with a programmatic question, a supposed
panacea for the alleged evils of unemployment and overpopulation.
Even so, no Puerto Rican official *publicly* admits the promotion
of emigration. On the contrary, Governor Hernández Colón, in his "El
Estado del País" (The State of the Country) message, delivered before
the Legislative Houses at the beginning of 1973, stressed that the
Governor of the "Free Associated State" of Puerto Rico neither
encouraged nor impeded the emigration of Puerto Ricans. This cutting
declaration of the governor deserves to be compared with the documents circulated among the agricultural workers of the interior of
Puerto Rico, stamped with the seal of the Department of Labor of the
"Free Associated State." For example, one of the documents circulated
said: "All those unemployed agricultural workers interested in going to
work in the farms of the United States under contract with the
Department of Labor of Puerto Rico are advised that we have worker
recruitment." Another document, dated March 27, 1972, indicates that
the representatives of the owners of Shade Tobacco Growers and
Garden State Cooperative have expressed to the Department of Labor
"their urgent need to get workers in sufficient quantity in order to be
able to meet its calendar of flights scheduled for the beginning of
May."[5]

That, and that alone, is the simple truth with respect to Puerto
Rican emigration, in spite of the public pronouncements of the spokes-
men of our colonial elite. We have already referred to the famous report
to the Governor on "Opportunities of Employment, Education and
Training" (1973), where they speak in no uncertain terms about emigra-
tion as an "escape valve." The report is discussed in the presence of
Governor Hernández Colón in the same year in which Hernández
Colón reiterates, for the nth time, that his government neither promotes

nor discourages Puerto Rican emigration. History repeats itself. Twenty-six years before, some of the historic personages who were later to produce the 1973 report, sat down with another colonial governor to recommend what others are recommending twenty-five years later. Here is the eternal return, the no-exit street. Nothing has changed, everything goes on the same. Only the actors change while the protagonists play the same role as their predecessors.*

But let us return to the agricultural workers who have emigrated. Let us recall their condition as salaried workers who abandon their homes in the rural areas of Puerto Rico in order to work on the farms of the northeast of the United States. How does this process come about and what are its essential characteristics?

The already mentioned studies done by Professors Luis Nieves Falcón and Ricardo Puerta, as well as the evidence accumulated by the Division of Migrants of the Office of Legal Services of Puerto Rico, headed by Attorney Salvador Tío, Jr., offers us the following picture:

The process of recruiting agricultural workers begins typically by means of the intervention of a "Crew Leader" ("Líder de Brigadas"), who is generally from the neighborhood where the workers live and is in charge of contracting—verbally, most of the time, because the majority of the workers emigrate without the mediation of a formal contract—those interested in the available work. The salary offered to these workers is greater than the minimum salary prevailing in Puerto Rico. In 1972, for example, they were offered a salary of $2.25 an hour in the United States in contrast to $1.05 or up to $1.15 an hour in Puerto Rico. They are also offered payment of the costs for air and land travel to the places where they will work. Once recruited in sufficient numbers, the agricultural workers are taken to the airport where they board the plane to their destinations under the suspicious eyes of the crew leaders. When they arrive on U.S. territory (let's say, in this case, New York City), the *braceros* are immediately loaded onto buses or trucks which take them to their respective farms. This involves several hours of passage on highways and roads unknown to the emigrant, a person who, as a general rule, has barely left the rural area from which he hails in Puerto Rico.

*It is still interesting to see the presence of Mr. Teodoro Moscoso in both groups and occasions (1948 and 1973). Mr. Moscoso is, without doubt, one of the most important colonial hierarchs. His longevity at the service of "good causes"—like that of Puerto Rican emigration—is already almost proverbial.

Puerto Rican *braceros* are generally quartered in wooden shacks, where the sanitation facilities, heating and recreation facilities are—if they exist at all—extremely limited. The food is equally deficient, in spite of the requirements to the contrary in the laws and rules regarding the treatment of migrant workers.

Professor Ricardo Puerta offers us the following picture of working conditions of Puerto Rican migrant workers in these agricultural consortiums:

> The working day of the migrant exceeds forty hours a week, without these extra hours bringing in extra compensation (over-time); rather, he receives normal pay. Normally, work begins between six and seven o'clock in the morning and ends between four and five in the afternoon. Since the day is longer in the summer, one could work up until eight o'clock at night if the circumstances so required, although such practice is rather rare. At noon, there is a free hour for lunch. Saturday is a work day and it is probable that during the harvesting one will also work Sundays. The longest work week given by a Puerto Rican was seventy hours, but the most often repeated one was fifty to sixty hours weekly . . .
>
> It is evident that the agricultural worker cannot work every day even if he or she wanted to. The cold and rain, health factors and the unforeseen factors of a highly mechanized agriculture are obstacles to the flow of continual daily work.
>
> As a result, there are low work weeks for one reason or another. Considering these weeks and balancing them with those of full-time work, it would not be venturous to estimate that in 1970 a migrant who has finished the season averaged a net salary of $80.00 weekly during his stay in New York State. If we accepted such an averaged estimate and we multiplied it by the 28 weeks a season lasts, we could say that, in the most successful cases of the migratory cycle, the worker without contract only accumulates $2,240.00 as net salary during his stay outside Puerto Rico. From this amount he and his family have to live, at the human cost of being separated for more than half a year.[6]

As the reader will note, the average salary of the worker is dramatically reduced, even considering the great difference that exists between the worker's salary in the United States and the salary he would have earned had he remained on the Island. Add to this the fact that, at the end of his stay in the United States, he discovers that the price of his plane ticket has been deducted from his salary, that all his purchases of clothing, drinks, cigarettes, entertainment, etc., have to be made through the agricultural consortium's stores, and that his ability to move freely has been radically limited. Still more, once inside the farm, the Puerto Rican worker cannot leave it without the expressed authorization of the employer. Any violation of this rule runs serious risks. For example, the police authorities bordering the agricultural camps collaborate with the farmers to prevent the possible "flight" of the emigrants. It should be noted that the immense majority of these workers do not know English, nor are they familiar with their environment. If the police surprise them outside the boundaries of the farm, they can be arrested for violation of the "vagrancy laws." This means that they will spend the night in jail until the employer is notified to come and get them. Even if he scoffs at this barrier by the local police, the worker confronts an additional difficulty: he does not have a return ticket to Puerto Rico. Besides, he does not know English and is generally unfamiliar with his whereabouts. This pathetic picture has been described, *lived* by thousands of Puerto Rican workers.

Given these circumstances, we do not consider it an exaggeration to assert that the conditions prevailing on U.S. agricultural farms border on involuntary servitude. In fact, there have been the public exposure of several recent cases that illustrate these coercive practices which constitute the daily burden of our compatriots on these farms. A concentration camp atmosphere exists in the camps of the agricultural workers. This is shown by Dr. Luis Nieves Falcón's most recent study on this subject. We say this not to aggravate passions, but rather to describe a reality.

Recently, concrete instances of the mistreament and of the involuntary servitude to which Puerto Rican *braceros* are subjected in the United States captured public attention. One of the latest examples is that of ten *Boricuan* minors who were recruited illegally to work in the Coz Farms fields of South Carolina. These minors were offered $150.00 a week and the opportunity to return to Puerto Rico when they wanted. But according to the testimony of the minors, as described by Attorney Salvador Tío, Jr., this is what really happened:

> During the first two weeks, after 96 hours, the minors in question had not received any pay. Canales (the recruiter) deducted from their pay money to cover the expenses incurred by him for transportation, food and other entertainment expenses. Besides not receiving any pay for their work during these weeks, the minors were threatened by Canales, who kept a good number of firearms hoarded in the camp, warning them that if they left or tried to escape from the camp, he would take drastic action against them.[7]

Even though it cannot be proven that all Puerto Rican agricultural workers are subjected to an analogous treatment by the agricultural companies that contract them, there can be no doubt that the legal as well as the cultural safeguards that could serve as brakes against such mistreatment of people are scarce. The emigrant agricultural worker is the worker least protected by work laws, both in the metropolis and in Puerto Rico. His legal defenselessness unquestionably contributes to his condition of impotence before the boss. With respect to legal protection for agricultural workers, Gary S. Goodpastor, Professor of Law at the University of Iowa, concludes the following:

> The chief determinants of the actual working conditions in which agricultural labor finds itself are not found in the statutes, but in migrancy, underemployment, poverty, the existence of a surplus labor pool of agricultural workers, and the nature of agricultural economies and the agricultural market. Economic efficiency, where there is a substantial job competition and grossly inadequate information about jobs and working conditions, operates to keep labor costs low, whether such costs are in the form of wages, housing or safety and health precautions in the fields. Such laws as exist to protect the farmworker in the relatively unregulated farm labor economy tend to be ineffective. Whether wage, housing, or health and safety laws, the same reasons for ineffectiveness appear: regulatory agencies tend to be locally controlled by the employer and operate to serve his interest; there is inadequate funding; enforcement staffs are small and lack autonomous sanctioning authority; ethnic, racial, social class, and educational differences operate to the disadvantage of agricultural workers. More fundamentally, however, regulatory legislation violates one of the fundamental rubrics regarding the control of human behavior, well articulated by Rousseau: never separate a man's duty from his interest. At present, there are a few good economic reasons for farm employers to increase wages and improve working conditions for farmworkers. At the same time, reducing costs is always a good economic reason not to do so.

> In other areas of concern, authorities responsible for providing social welfare services—such as welfare, food, health, and educational services— to farmworkers are often inadequately prepared and organized. Programs are often not sufficiently comprehensive and coherent, and there is too little coordination and mutual planning by Federal, State, and local agencies and officials responsible for administering programs relating to farmworkers. Local administration of such programs is often parsimonious and impossibly bureaucratic. The overall impression which arises from a reading of the literature and from observation of the operation of programs for farmworkers is that even well-intentioned efforts to assist them are but inefficient and sporadic interventions conducted by a very complex, disorganized, and poorly coordinated social service network easily confused, diverted, bogged down, and exhausted. These services, highly important notwithstanding the great inadequacies, are not reaching the real problems of migratory and seasonal farmworkers in any substantial way.[8]

In spite of the protests by the authorities of the "Associated Free State," the lack of effective and efficient legal protection for Puerto Rican agricultural workers continues. Those who emigrate without their signature on a contract with the agricultural consortiums continue to flood the metropolis. Up until the present moment in which we are writing (1975), the Secretary of Labor has not met the obligation imposed by Law 87 of 1962 to establish the minimum guarantees that should guide the contracting of *Boricuan* agricultural workers by U.S. companies. This dereliction of duty on the part of the Secretary of Labor reduces the *Boricuan* agricultural workers to the level of peons, lacking the most elementary protections and rights to which they are entitled as Puerto Ricans and as human beings. But none of this should surprise us, now that we have seen how the mass emigration of Puerto Ricans to the metropolis is a process favored by the Governor of Puerto Rico himself.

We are forced to conclude this chapter with some observations with respect to the relation between emigrant Puerto Rican agricultural workers and other agricultural workers from Mexico and Central America, the West Indies, the Dominican Republic and Haiti, etc. It is important to observe the fact that agricultural workers—whether or not they are Puerto Rican and, therefore, U.S. citizens—suffer the most impoverished working conditions, while at the same time lacking the power of collective bargaining which the existence of unions in their work centers could provide. Add to this the lack of laws that protect, albeit minimally, the most elementary social rights of these workers and we will better understand how these great contingents of the human labor force suffer the most pitiless exploitation at the hands of those big capitalists in agriculture. We note therefore a kind of mass evacuation of thousands and thousands of workers who live at the subsistence level and who flow back and forth throughout the entire Caribbean and Central America in desperate search for a means of survival. Multinational corporations such as Gulf and Western attract and then release contingents of Haitians and Dominicans according to the work force needs of their farms in the Dominican Republic or in the United States. We see therefore the migratory flow of Haitian sugar cane cutters to the Dominican Republic, Dominican workers risking their lives to enter Puerto Rico illegally to work for whatever they are paid, Puerto Ricans who emigrate to the metropolis because there are no job opportunities for them in Puerto Rico, etc. In the metropolis, we also see *braceros* arriving from Jamaica, Mexico, and Central America; in short, a human work force traffic that responds to the contradictions and expansions of capitalist economy is becoming more firmly established. The very abundance of this work force maintains salaries at subsistence levels. We see, therefore, how surplus value is extracted from human labor under the most inhuman conditions conceivable. The Caribbean, therefore—with the sole exception of Cuba—is the great reserve of a cheap and abundant labor force that nourishes U.S. monopoly capital in accordance with its moments of prosperity and crisis. The problem is not one that can be circumscribed within a national scale, but rather it takes on an international dimension. In the same way that monopoly capital breaks national barriers and attempts to integrate the world within its global scope, so too the proletariat necessarily assumes a dimension which transcends national contexts. Therefore, there is no doubt at all that the problem of the exploitation of agricultural workers—whether they be Puerto Rican, Chicano, Jamaican or Portuguese—can only be fully resolved when the social and economic structures of the world capitalist process have been abolished and surpassed.

*The ideas of the ruling class are in every
epoch the ruling ideas, i.e., the class which is
the ruling material force of society is at the
same time its ruling intellectual force.*
KARL MARX

6

THE PROBLEM OF
CULTURAL ASSIMILATION

Puerto Rico is a society with a national culture tied historically,
ethnically, and linguistically to the Latin American cultural universe
and, more specifically, to the area of the Spanish-speaking Caribbean.
In another, but similar context, we said that:

> If by culture we are to understand here the entire spiritual creation of a
> society, meaning all that wealth of ideas and beliefs, habits and customs,
> artifacts and additional qualities that characterize it, then it is this zone of
> collective life that the colonizers will observe with greed in their attempt to
> penetrate this spiritual creation, by reducing to a minimum its capacity to
> resist, by converting that autochthonous culture into a mere adornment
> without content.[1]

The cultural history of Puerto Rico since the military occupation
of Puerto Rico by U.S. troops in 1898 offers indisputable proof to
corroborate this thesis. Recent studies by prominent linguists and
educators such as Drs. Aida Negrón de Montilla, Silvia Viera, Germán
de Granda Gutiérrez and Elizier Narváez serve to substantiate our
arguments. Twentieth century Puerto Rican society has been victimized by a merciless siege[2] which, although it has not been able to
dissolve the most profound features of our cultural activity, has succeeded nevertheless, in having an effect on the process through which
our people are historically and culturally tied to Latin American
peoples. In other words, present-day Puerto Rican society encounters
the blows of a systematic process of cultural assimilation which can
take place—and in fact *is* taking place—perfectly in the Spanish

language. We are dealing not only with the conservation of the vernacular as a simple means of communication, but rather with the absorption
and adoption by important population sectors—especially the middle
strata—of the values and world-view characteristic of U.S. capitalism.
Given this, the process of cultural assimilation in Puerto Rico cannot be
seen unconnected to either the class structure of Puerto Rican society,
the function of Spanish and English in the daily life of these classes, or
the way class position determines both the perceptions of the metropolis and the metropolis-colony political relationship.

The points just made are relevant because among Puerto Rican
intellectual circles there has existed a very pronounced tendency to
contrast the degree of cultural assimilation suffered by our compatriots
in the United States to the alleged—or real—Puerto Rican cultural
affirmation in the midst of this siege. It has even been held that Puerto
Ricans born in the United States have ceased to be Puerto Rican and
that, therefore, they should be considered dead weight, which has
already broken off all relations with our society. We believe that the
question is very serious and ought to be discussed in depth.

Let us proceed by parts. Not long ago we defined culture as a
homeless reality, very much like a world-view that allows us to define
and determine precisely a society's profile. Let us be even more precise.
Culture in itself is a class phenomenon, that is, a social reality that can
only be understood by beginning with the relations of production in a
society at a determined historic moment. The main conception of the
world, the value-giving views, the very perception of the natural, social
and cultural world all take place within this context. This has a double
application for our society: we are dealing with some relations of
production that are the product of both colonialism and capitalism.
And added to the exploitation, which is natural to capitalism, is the
"inferiorization," which is coessential to colonialism. In any case, we
understand that Puerto Rican emigration to the United States deepens
and aggravates this problem, but it should not be considered something
qualitatively different from the cultural reality of the Island. The
cultural differences—especially with respect to the problem of language—between Puerto Ricans who live in Puerto Rico and those who
reside in the United States are differences of degree rather than of
nature.

Let us begin by seeing things from the perspective of Puerto Ricans
in the United States. The basic unit of our analysis will be the Puerto

Rican population where it is found to be concentrated in the greatest number, that is, in New York City. Let us conceive of this city as a kind of model or paradigm, where the cultural problems of U.S. society can be seen with greater clarity and precision.

Now let us think about a child born of Puerto Rican parents in New York during the postwar period. Compare the cultural condition of this child to that of a child born under similar conditions in Puerto Rico. It will be evident, before we go on, that the comparison would be inaccurate and dishonest if we compared the cultural condition of a child born in a New York ghetto to one who is born to the Puerto Rican petty bourgeoisie. It would be even more inaccurate if we overlooked the sociological fact that the social composition of the Puerto Rican population in the United States is predominantly one of proletarian character. The problem of cultural assimilation cannot be seen independently from the question of class.

The first thing we should observe in this context is that the categorical imperative of cultural life in the metropolis is assimilation or integration with respect to the values, world view and *language* of U.S. society. Ideologues like Nathan Glazer and Daniel Patrick Moynihan have tried to elaborate a new theory about race relations in the United States. *Beyond the Melting Pot,* the title of one book published by these authors, gives the essence of their ideology.[3] The objective of this ideology is to go beyond the old thesis that the United States is a melting pot of nationalities, projecting a concept according to which a new synthesis seems to emerge which nullifies and at the same time goes beyond the melting pot. Nevertheless, these same authors are forced to admit that every ethnic group which has just arrived in the United States is still expected to come close to "the Anglo Saxon center," that is, to subordinate its own characteristics and culture to the values of a society dominated by "Anglos."

Some contemporary essayists have severely criticized this ideological thesis, which argues that ethnic groups of non-European origin only have to pass through a process of initiation and adjustment similar to that which Europeans suffer in order to be socially and culturally admitted into U.S. society. On the contrary, some of them have pointed out the differences between the treatment received by the European emigrants from the north of the old continent and that of those immigrants coming from the south of that same region. There is a sharp distinction between European immigration and that phenomenon resulting from transplanting of human contingents for slavery purposes (as in the case of the Afro-American population),[4] as well as that of Mexicans, Asians, West Indians, Puerto Ricans, etc. Racist practices, so prevalent in the United States, have increased, and the assimilation and integration of these ethnic groups into U.S. capitalist society have become extremely difficult, if not impossible. It is necessary to observe the contradiction in this society of its alleged capacity to assimilate ethnic groups socially classified as "non-white," and the persistent rejection of these groups by considering them "inferior." From the Native American Indians, who originally populated the continent, up through our recently arrived compatriots, the prevailing factor has always been the ominous presence of racism. The Puerto Rican anthropologist, Dr. Eduardo Seda Bonilla, makes some observations about racism and its effects on Puerto Rican emigrants which deserve to be quoted extensively. Dr. Seda Bonilla tells us:

> No matter how fallacious, for example, it may be to talk about a Jewish race or a Puerto Rican race, or of a pure race, in the biological sense, the important social fact is that these social myths have determined in the past (as in the case of the Jews of Nazi Germany) and determine in the present (in the case of the Puerto Ricans in New York), a social position of discrimination for those culturally unified populations. . . .

> The criterion of social identity on the basis of characteristics socially defined as belonging to a social type constitutes one of the most strongly sanctioned criteria in the North American social structure. People classified in the social group of the "white population" enjoy a margin of prestige, life opportunities and political power which contrast sharply to that of the population classified as black. In the socio-racial North American structure, life opportunities, such as the kind of jobs, salaries and working conditions, the kind of housing, respect and dignity—or, instead, ignominy and rebuke—in interpersonal relations, are determined in great part by the socio-racial "status" in which the individual is located in the caste structure.[5]

It is important to stress this question because it is one of the most serious problems that confronts the Puerto Ricans in the United States. This is even more so for Black Puerto Ricans who emigrate or who have been born in the metropolis. The Black Puerto Rican who goes to the United States confronts a racial prejudice of such virulence and intensity that it makes the racism that admittedly prevails in Puerto Rico look pale by comparison.[6]

But the Black Puerto Rican is not the only Puerto Rican who suffers this prejudice. As soon as they arrive in the metropolis, those who are considered "white" in Puerto Rico fall into a new racial category—that of non-whites. This novel and ingenious racial category places us in an unknown terrain equidistant from Blacks and whites. From the point of view of the class structure of the metropolis, the classification in question performs an important divisive function: instead of placing us alongside Afro-Americans, who are united with us by their common experience of slavery, as well as intermarriage, it opens a gap between *Boricuas* and Afro-Americans. What stands out, therefore, is not what unites both minority groups—exploitation and discrimination—but rather the alleged "color line" that separates us.

The race question is at the same time designed to cloud the problem of class, which constitutes that most important common denominator that we share with all ethnic groups not of European origin. U.S. society is divided into classes, and, in determining the class position of each person, the factor of race or ethnic origin plays a dominant role. So, for example, in social mobility and access to the material and spiritual goods of this society, ethnic origin is of capital importance. For many children of European immigrants—especially those who come from the south of Europe—to ascend the social ladder has meant changing their last names by making them "Anglo". (Let us take the case of prominent contemporary politicians like Barry Goldwasser, or Goldwater, and Spiro Agnoustoupoulos, or Agnew). But in the case of African, Asian or Caribbean emigrants, the racial factor prevails. A Puerto Rican whose last name is Ríos can easily change himself into a Rivers, but his ethnic mark is less eraseable than that of an immigrant of European origin.

Let us return to our Puerto Rican child. If we are to analyze correctly the class position of Puerto Ricans in the United States, we cannot deny that the vast majority of them belong to the working class (industrial or, in the case of agricultural workers, rural). The typical Puerto Rican child, therefore, comes from a social class that has not had access to higher education, that is often unemployed and that is daily victimized by institutionalized racial prejudice in U.S. capitalist society.

Now let us examine the cultural context within which he moves from the very moment in which the process of socialization begins. The first thing we must observe is an indisputable sociological fact: to be Puerto Rican in the United States means to belong to what the ruling class calls an "ethnic minority." Puerto Ricans in the United States *are* in fact a minority within U.S. society. A very important cultural fact is derived from this: every "ethnic minority" must, through a political-cultural imperative, be assimilated into U.S. culture. Assimilation in this context is synonymous with "North-Americanization." As professor Milton Gordon pointed out in his important study:

> If there is anything in American life which can be described as an over-all American culture which serves as a reference point for immigrants and their children, it can best be described, it seems to us, as the middle-class cultural patterns of, largely, white Protestant, Anglo-Saxon origins, . . .

> Given the prior arrival time of the English colonists, the numerical dominance of the English stock, and the cultural dominance of Anglo-Saxon institutions, the invitation extended to non-English immigrants to "melt" could only result, if thoroughly accepted, in the latter's loss of group identity, the transformation of their cultural survivals into Anglo-Saxon patterns, and the development of their descendants in the image of the Anglo-Saxon American.[7]

In the face of this indisputable social fact, the average Puerto Rican child begins his or her education in an inhospitable and hostile environment where the child's culture, history and language are usually denied and degraded by the educational authorities. In addition, the child's class origins also place the child in an extremely disadvantageous position. Under these circumstances, our child not only loses his language, in a society where English is the vernacular, but loses even his first name in the process, when at the very moment of his matriculation in school the child suffers a severe cultural mutilation: Ricardo is changed with a stroke of the pen to Richard, Juan to John. That is only the beginning of the socialization process which will revolve at every moment around the affirmation of the Anglo-Saxon worldview and the negation of the contributions of "inferior" peoples like us. The result of this is what we have expected: the average Puerto Rican child born and raised in the metropolis loses the use of his language or is able to speak it only with a great deal of difficulty, changing very often from English to Spanish and vice versa when conversing with others. This has brought about the rise of what some call "Spanglish," that is, a dialect that consists of Spanish-izing words taken from English. (So, for example, pochó = pork chops; yardita = yard; furnitura = furniture; rufa = roof, etc.)[8]

The severity of the situation is illustrated by the fact that the average Puerto Rican child winds up in a kind of no-man's land, where his command of English is as problematic as his knowledge of Spanish. Due to the continual flow of emigrants, a considerable number of children born in Puerto Rico suffer from sudden cultural transplantation to the metropolis. Naturally, these children have no knowledge of the English language. On the other hand, the majority of the children born in the metropolis are raised in communities where the Spanish language—in spite of the process of dissolution and corruption to which it has been subjected—still predominates in daily conversations, music, business, etc. Studies on the New York City educational system indicate that over 250,000 Puerto Rican students attend the city schools—one-fourth of the city's total school registration. Of this number, it is estimated that some 100,000 have problems with English. As one can observe, this is equivalent to a little less than half of all Puerto Rican students. Given this reality, the following picture is more easily understood: 86 percent of Puerto Rican children are found to be below the normal reading level, and the school drop-out rate is the worst in the city (57 percent), compared to 46 percent for Black students and 29 percent for other students. Moreover, only 15 percent of Puerto Ricans over twenty-five years of age have obtained a high school diploma, compared to 53.4 percent of whites of the same age.[9]

Racial and social prejudice, which is institutionalized in U.S. capitalist society, uses these figures in turn as proof of the "mental retardation" of Puerto Ricans. The fact is that, upon being subjected to such an intense process of cultural privation, this proposition turns into what some sociologists call the "self-fulfilling prophecy." Or rather, it states that Puerto Ricans are "inferior" because they do not reach the education levels of whites and other ethnic groups which have assimilated the values of the United States. This is also the reason why Puerto Ricans will never be able to be "true" North Americans nor reach the educational levels of "true" North Americans: the very educational system is responsible for having placed us in such a disadvantageous position that we are condemned to failure even before we begin the struggle. In this vicious circle, the Puerto Rican population is plunged into a dead-end alley, which turns radically limits the chances of the young Puerto Rican from the ghetto to transcend his social environment. Given that situation, the creed of equality upon which U.S. capitalist society is supposedly based is seen for what it really is: a myth which has been skillfully plotted to conceal the true nature of power relations in the metropolis.

As a consequence, we find a problem which is somewhat unusual in its cultural ramifications: our Puerto Rican brothers and sisters residing in the United States—especially the more recent generations—do not have even an elementary command of either Spanish or English. It is often said that this is because they are bilingual, but this statement is only partially true. If by bilingual one means a person who speaks both languages fluently, then this is definitely not the case of Puerto Ricans who live in the United States. The language of the United States is English. A considerable proportion of Puerto Ricans who live in New York City, according to what we have seen, do not know this language. They are more familiar, although with difficulty, with the Spanish language. Perhaps it would be better to describe them as "nonlingual" instead of bilingual or monolingual, were it not for the fact that our compatriots evidently seek their own means of expression, manners and tonalities that allow them to leap, dialectically, from a linguistic no-man's land to an arena in which they are able to communicate within their own ethnic group. Be that as it may, the situation is horrible. It is horrible not according to mere Spanish linguistic purity, but because of the terrible mutilation that this idiomatic ambivalence implies, the dreadful reality that condemns us to the category of cultural pariahs in the metropolis as well as in the colony.

To a great degree, this fact has led to an attempt to coin a new term capable of defining the Puerto Rican born and raised in New York. We are dealing with an allegedly new cultural category: that of the "New Yorricans" or "New Ricans" or "Ricans." The precise name matters little. What is important is the reality it attempts to describe. The fact of the matter is that the author at least is unfamiliar with the origin of the term "New Yorrican" which has become so generalized today. But he does know the profound cultural and political implications of this classification. We are dealing, no more and no less, with creating a new cultural category somewhere between Puerto Rican and U.S. American, a kind of cultural hybrid similar to the Mexican *pachuco* so masterfully described by Octavio Paz in *The Labyrinth of Solitude*.

Dr. Eduardo Seda Bonilla clearly defines the problem from this perspective:

> The real fact is that many Puerto Rican immigrants have lost their cultural roots through acculturation in the first generation, or through the natural process of enculturation in the second generation, and they are Puerto Rican only according to North American cultural guidelines which define the

identity of individuals on the basis of "race." They are defined as Puerto Ricans because they belong to an alleged Puerto Rican race which is not white in its genetic composition. From this racist classification, behavior is explained as actualization inherent to "racial" condition. This conceptualization of Puerto Rican-ness based on American racism makes the New Yorrican a human being marginal to two cultures. From the Yankee cultural perspective, the New Yorrican understands that we Puerto Ricans constitute a "race" and that Puerto Rican behavior is a product of that "race," and he presumes to be Puerto Rican by virtue of belonging to the race in question. In other words, the New Yorrican is the product of a paradox. American racism, to which he is exposed in his enculturation, in order to reject him converts him into a "Puerto Rican." The same racism that places him in that position prevents him from seeing that the language of Puerto Ricans is Spanish, even though the New Yorrican generally does not speak Spanish, or else he speaks it with difficulty. The same cultural loss of vision prevents him from seeing that his values are the values of North Americans, that his vision of reality and of his future is that of North Americans, that his being has been molded within North American cultural perimeters except as self-fulfilling prophecy. In the face of this paradoxical disjuncture, the New Yorrican has the option of taking his Puerto Rican-ness in the same way the Chicanos take their Mexican-ness, or Blacks their African-ness, or Italian-Americans their Italian-ness, or of taking seriously a process of inverse acculturation towards the authentic roots of the culture to which he says he belongs.[10]

The problem with this interpretation, and others analogous to it, is that it presents as already consummated a cultural fact whose consummation is intrinsically problematic, and whose political implications cannot in any way escape serious study. According to the fatalistic perspective of Dr. Seda Bonilla, the die is already cast for the people he and others call "New Yorricans." The question we must ask is: do we declare, therefore, that those young people born in the United States are not Puerto Rican, and that, therefore, they belong to a new cultural species?

We refuse to accept this thesis. We refuse because if we did accept it, we would be supporting the idea that the new Puerto Rican generations born in the metropolis have already ceased to constitute an integrated and integral part of Puerto Rican national culture. On the contrary, both our personal experience and our social investigations indicate that among young Puerto Ricans born in the United States during the postwar period, there exists a profound desire to identify themselves with what is Puerto Rican, to affirm their national roots. That this affirmation may generally be expressed and embraced in English does not prevent the young Puerto Rican from affirming himself by rejecting attempts to make him what he definitely does not feel he is: North American.

The primary contention of this work is that the difference between the U.S. attempts at cultural assimilation in Puerto Rico and in the metropolis is one of degree and not of type, and that the process in the metropolis simply takes a more enslaving, smashing monolithic character than is the case in the colony. In order to examine this problem, it seems to me that we ought to refer to the process of cultural assimilation exactly as it is manifested not in the metropolis but on the island of Puerto Rico.

Professor Pedro Juan Rúa, in an article published recently in the journal *Nueva Lucha,* hit the nail on the head by calling the process that Puerto Rican society suffers on the cultural level a process of "deculturation." It should be noted that we are not dealing with a mere semantic distinction. With this term Rúa offers us the profound dimension of the problem by means of the prefix "de," which, in a context like the present one, can only mean the negation of Puerto Rican culture, its being uprooted and crushed in the face of the hegemonic culture imposed by imperialism. The question is posed in its proper perspective when seen as an ideological problem, as observed by Marx in *The German Ideology:*

> The ideas of the ruling class are in every epoch the ruling ideas, i.e., the class which is the ruling *material* force of society is at the same time its ruling *intellectual* force. The class which has the means of material production at its disposal, has control at the same time over the means of mental production, so that thereby, generally speaking, the ideas of those who lack the means of mental production are subject to it. The ruling ideas are nothing more than the ideal expression of the dominant material relationships, the dominant material relationships grasped as ideas; hence of the relationships which make the one class the ruling one, therefore, the ideas of its dominance. The individuals composing the ruling class possess among other things consciousness and therefore think. Insofar, therefore, as they rule as a class and determine the extent and compass of an epoch, it is self-evident that they do this in its whole range, hence among other things rule also as thinkers, as producers of ideas, and regulate the production and distribution of the ideas of their age: thus their ideas are the ruling ideas of the epoch.[11]

In present-day Puerto Rican society, the ideas of the ruling class are those that correspond to the concept of the world and the values imposed by the metropolis' monopolist ruling class. The weak and parasitic Puerto Rican bourgeoisie is dedicated to grotesque imitation of that world vision. The reluctant defense that this bourgeoisie often makes of Spanish as "our language" is a last rampart of resistence that sounds hollow before the incredible avalanche of publicity which is daily poured on our people through all the mass media. Given these circumstances, it is not strange that Spanish itself is becoming more and more impoverished as a language within our own borders, nor that we have to lament the emergence of a new generation of Puerto Ricans, which Professor Luis Rafael Sánchez has perceptively called the *"Generation of O Sea."** In that context, linguistic interference has altered the face of Spanish[12] in Puerto Rico equally in both its form and content. We are not saying that we Puerto Ricans speak a kind of *patois* Spanish, but the influence of the English language on our daily life is very profound, and as a result there has been a systematic process of impoverishment of Spanish in our homeland. Professor Luis Rafael Sánchez, in the article just cited, excellently points out to us:

> I write in Puerto Rican when I say that among us the language is not managed with comfort, agility or perfection, nor with the ease and zeal of someone for whom the language is not cause for tension but rather the vehicle that transmits his intimate vibrations: the spiritual, the ideal, the material. Listen! I'm not referring to a language of distorted idioms or battered purisms, resplendent with shawls, castanets and Castillian Z's that burst your ears. Nor am I referring to a language of buried classist intention and fragmentary anthology-like erudition with which one travels through the academics of arts and sciences, the decrees of civic clubs and the telluric poetry of lyrical idiocy which has had such a long career among us. I am speaking of the awkwardness of organizing experiences from the ordinary, vigrous word; I am speaking of the difficulties of a firm, profound, clear possession of our language, our only language, in spite of the bureaucratic lie of bilingualism.

> This hesitation to name things, this resorting to the mercy of the "That is to say" translator of a thought that is never expressed, this substitution of real words for grotesquely manufactured terms like *el DESO, la DESA, el COSO, el COSITO ESE, la COSITA ESA, la VAINA ESA, el APARATITO QUE ES COMO UNA COSITA REDONDITA,*** all this has a clear explanation: it is the result of the ambivalent colonized and colonizing education at the simultaneous levels of both home and school.*

But we do not want to hammer this obvious point into the ground.

O Sea, a short expression in Spanish, meaning "rather," "that is to say," etc.
**Spanish terms with approximate colloquial or slang English translations such as: "stuff," "gadget," "thingumabob," "thingumajig," "doodad," "dohickey," "gismo," "whatchamacallit," "something or other," etc.

Let us return to the ideological point. If this focus is correct then we can only conclude that capitalist ideology dominates wherever capitalism is the hegemonic system and that this ideology has, therefore, an international or global character. In the same way in which capitalism seeks to extend and expand with the objective of integrating greater portions of the world into its division of labor and its world market, so too will it extend its ideological nets to the most remote confines of the earth. In that process, capitalism seeks to subject the autochthonous culture to a standard of cultural homogenization, that is, it seeks to maintain the form of the traditional or national cultures while injecting into them *the content* of the values and world outlook of capitalism. Once the objective is achieved, they can easily praise and even glorify the "picturesque" or archaic aspects of a cultural formation, while they go on to strip this formation of any real and effective connection with the authentically popular roots of the community.

We believe, therefore, that the Puerto Rican cultural problem both in the United States and in Puerto Rico should be analyzed from three levels inextricably linked by the very dynamics of contemporary capitalist society: the international level, the level of the metropolis' society and the level of the colonial society.

As far as the international level is concerned, I think that we should emphasize the process of homogenization of national cultures under the stamp of world capitalism. From this perspective, imperialism seeks to *integrate* all these diverse cultures with the stamp of the capitalist world outlook. Since diversity in languages, customs, dress, etc. could not be eliminated without finding a strong resistance among the affected peoples, they seek to use that diversity by exaltation of the exotic or the folkloric, while they penetrate or try to penetrate into the deepest strata of the collective consciousness by means of the uniforming standard of bourgeois values. So, the forms of national cultures are maintained—their external aspects—while they are emptied of all *substance*. Once imperialism has reached that objective, the process of cultural penetration begins to bear fruit. Corín Tellado and the *Reader's Digest, Superman* and *Donald Duck, Mission Impossible* and *Mod Squad* are translated and propagated in many languages with one identical message. Don Quijote's route is lined with Coca Cola ads. As Armand Mattelart has so perceptively indicated:

> Every economic and juridic mythology—which Marx disemboweled—that permits the ruling class to control the people's means of existence, has

welcomed still another mythical body with the development of what could be considered a new *productive force*: the mass means of communication. This new force is the technological power of manipulation and indoctrination: the control of consciousness through the daily and mass legitimation of the power bases of a class.[13]

In that global level of mass communication, Puerto Rican society is subjected to a process of cultural aggression very similar to that which other societies suffer under the capitalist cultural orbit. Within the diversity, we find therefore a common denominator: the bourgeois ideology that plans to dominate the social pyramid from the top to the base.

On a second level we find the great metropolis of world capitalism, the United States of America. As we previously stressed, the fundamental values of U.S. society are those of the ruling capitalist class. The process of cultural homogenization is carried out in this context as part of the messianic and racist conception that is expressed through the predominance of the Anglo ruling circles. Conformism and cultural integration of the values and world outlook of U.S. capitalist society are manifested through the cultural destruction of all the immigrant nationalities throughout the history of this common denominator of "North Americanization." From that point of view, U.S. society forces every immigrant group to submit to the experience of eventually disappearing as a national group, although this group may maintain the paraphernalia of its national origin. In the United States, there does not exist such a thing as cultural pluralism. Yet that cultural pluralism is precisely what seems to be promoted at the international level, within the cultural orbit of imperialism, although we have seen how a unified and integrated substratum of the bourgeois world-view is found lying under that pluralism. Within U.S. society, nevertheless, there is no way out: cultural integration and assimilation only spare from their clutches those peripheral aspects of the national culture which U.S. society intends to integrate. Given these circumstances, Puerto Rican culture in the United States is confronted with an enslaving cultural offensive. In order to survive culturally, our brothers and sisters in the metropolis count primarily on their continual contact with the Island and with the diverse manifestations of Puerto Rican cultural affirmation which go from "salsa" music to protest poetry. But living in the very guts of the most powerful capitalist society cannot help but produce a group of people who want to "pass" into the society of the metropolis, even at the cost of losing their identity and national culture. This process of "de-

Puerto Ricanization" takes place at the same time as the process of
"Puerto Ricanization" or Puerto Rican affirmation, whose main protagonists are Puerto Rican youths born in the United States during the
post-World War II period. The dialectical development of the struggle
between these two tendencies is still uncertain, but there is no doubt
that the essence of the Puerto Rican cultural question in the metropolis
will depend on which of the two tendencies prevails. This in turn will
depend on international and national circumstances and events difficult to predict in this moment in which we are living.

On the third level, we have Puerto Rican culture in Puerto Rico.
Naturally, we cannot even talk about this subject in a political and
cultural vacuum. Puerto Rican national culture is inextricably connected to the international reality and to events in the metropolis. As an
integral part of that world which is subjected to the process of homogenization, all of Puerto Rican society is forced to yield to cultural
assimilation and integration, into the ideology of the metropolis. The
condition is further aggravated when we take into consideration the
colonial character of our society. As a consequence, we Puerto Ricans
suffer from the cultural assimilation of the world vision of the metropolis to a more intense and penetrating degree than does, for example, the
Dominican Republic; but this difference is one relative to the *intensity*
of cultural aggression and not to the nature itself of this aggression. We
are saying the same thing with respect to the problem of cultural
assimilation of Puerto Ricans in the United States.

To sum up, the problem of the cultural assimilation of Puerto
Ricans both in the metropolis and on the island of Puerto Rico itself
escapes facile definitions and mechanical slogans. We are dealing with
an extraordinarily complex question whose future unraveling will
depend first of all on political factors. Up until now, Puerto Ricans—
both those who live in Puerto Rico and those who live in the United
States—have demonstrated an extraordinary power of resistance in the
face of the repeated imperialist attempts to take away their culture and
language. But it is fitting to ask if this resistance will be effective for
much longer in the context of colonialism and neocolonialism. The
almost complete defenselessness of Puerto Ricans in the face of this
cultural aggression, a defenselessness brought about by the lack of the
most elementary rights and powers that mark the self-determination of
all peoples, unquestionably aggravates the problem we have posed.
Only a Puerto Rican revolution worthy of its name would be able to

break with the vicious circle of colonialism, by rescuing our material and spiritual heritage and eliminating bourgeois classculture from our society. A revolution of this kind, capable of placing culture within reach of the people and the people within reach of culture, would resolve the posed dillemma and would place us as a people within the great world current of triumphant socialism. This new synthesis would serve as a kind of principal factor in the redefinition of Puerto Rican culture within an internationalist and proletarian framework. It would then not be the stultifying culture of the elites, but rather a vigorous and living culture forged by the inhabitant of the New York ghetto and the peasant who picks coffee on the plantations of Yauco in their daily tasks.

But until that day arrives, it is our obligation to fight day by day, so that the right of our people to be precisely that, *a people,* is respected: a people, a society with its own profile, a cultural entity that is projected and upheld firmly and proudly even in the very center of the metropolis.

In order to conclude these observations, it would be worthwhile to make reference to two recent events in the field of education which, without any doubt, form part of the whole process of cultural negation and affirmation which we have tried to analyze in these last pages. I am referring, in the first place, to the programs of Puerto Rican Studies created principally under the auspices of the City University of New York (CUNY) and, in the second place, to the programs of bilingual education which, created principally under the auspices of CUNY and secondary schools, were passed by the United States government in 1965. In both cases we are confronted with relatively analogous cultural problems, although these take place at different levels of the educational and cultural process. No study of the Puerto Rican cultural question can disregard the analysis of these two closely connected processes when grappling to understand this subject.

Let us take first the case of the programs of Puerto Rican Studies, which are functioning primarily within the academic premises of the City University of New York. According to a recent study, there were fourteen such programs placed under the classification of "ethnic studies" that were of a Hispanic nature in 1972.[14] It will be understood that the scope of these programs is numerically insignificant: they constitute a barely perceptible unit within the U.S. university system. These programs are also very recent creations, resulting from social and political fervor of the 1960s. In addition, it is fitting to point to the creation of the Center of Puerto Rican Studies, created under the auspices of the City University of New York and the Ford Foundation in 1973. It is actually a center of social research of the Puerto Rican reality, especially in the metropolis. The director of this center, Dr. Frank Bonilla, speaking about the problem as a whole, has said:

> Until the 1960's the Puerto Rican presence in the U.S. universities was, of course, barely noticeable. As regards the New York community, this presence was for all effects limited to a selective trickle through the municipal colleges. Thus the present Puerto Rican generation in U.S. colleges is by and large our first university generation.[15]

This should not surprise us in light of what already has been said about the cultural privation which Puerto Ricans suffer daily in the United States. From that point of view, the creation of programs of Puerto Rican Studies is without doubt an important act of cultural affirmation. It is true that these programs were won as a result of the fight for Afro-American Studies, when the struggle of Blacks for their most elementary human rights was at its zenith. It is true, also, that the programs of Puerto Rican Studies, from the first moment of their creation, were faced with the need to create a professional staff not only suitable and academically competent but also familiar and identified with the problems and vicissitudes of the Puerto Rican community in the United States. But it is not less true that these difficulties have been gradually overcome in the sociohistoric process itself.

Nevertheless, several matters that cannot be passed over in the discussion of this subject remain:

1) Once we entered the decade of the 1970s, the protest movement in the United States entered an ebbing phase. The revelations of Watergate gave us a mild indication of the repression unleashed against the protest movement under Nixon's administration. The important thing for us to note is that both the student movement and the Black movement have entered into a phase of activism far lower than that of 1960s. This signifies, in practical terms, a hardening of university authorities in the exercise of their prerogatives in the face of student demands. Add to that the present economic depression, and the precarious situation of the programs of Puerto Rican Studies will be better understood. As with the labor market, where the Puerto Rican is the first to be fired and the last to be hired, when there are budgetary cuts in the universities, the Puerto Rican programs are the primary candidates for the axe on the altars of so-called economizing. This is

even more true if we take into consideration that the U.S. ruling class is not interested in, or worse still, it sees negatively, the establishing of academic programs that contribute to the creation of a Puerto Rican national consciousness with a clear anti-imperialist orientation. Therefore, it is logical to expect repeated attempts to neutralize, phase out or even completely eliminate programs of Puerto Rican Studies and other analogous activities in the coming years. We have on the one hand, the ideological tendency that claims to expect that in the coming years there will be repeated endeavors within the category of Ethnic Studies. From this point of view, programs of Puerto Rican Studies would become one more among ethnic studies, greatly diluting their social and political impact upon being geared towards a kind of academic "melting pot." On the other hand, we see that the great majority of the programs mentioned have a professional and student staff with sharply leftist tendencies, something that goes against the grain of the tendency to "return to normality," which seems to be the present prescription in U.S. universities. We believe that both factors could converge in order to bring about the neutralization indicated above. Whether or not this will be consummated will depend on the militancy and the demands of the Puerto Rican community for the continuation of the programs exactly as they have been functioning until this moment.

2) The programs of Puerto Rican Studies have confronted, ever since their inception, a problem which Dr. Frank Bonilla, in the work quoted earlier, attributes to the lack of people with the "academic" qualifications required by the U.S. university system. We are referring, of course, to the problem of "academic credentials"—the Ph.D. or M.A. degree conferred by institutions of higher learning—which constitute the *sine qua non* for employment in the U.S. university. As we pointed out earlier the proportion of resident Puerto Ricans in the United States who obtain a degree higher than the B.A. degree is numerically insignificant. The alternative, naturally, would be to recruit university professors from the Island to do the actual teaching in the United States. But this alternative faces two difficulties: a) there exists a pronounced reluctance among "Puerto Ricans from over there" to accept "Puerto Ricans from here," many of whom are considered by "those from over there" to be elitist, bourgeois, unfamiliar with the Puerto Rican reality in the United States, opportunists, etc. b) On the other hand, the Puerto Ricans residing on the Island who could be willing to work culturally with the Puerto Rican community in the

United States are generally people who are reluctant to leave their teaching positions in Puerto Rico to settle in the metropolis. In other words, this conflict between "Puerto Ricans from over there" and "Puerto Ricans from here" is a conflict which has great repercussions with respect to the programs of Puerto Rican Studies, especially in New York City. Therefore a serious problem of communication exists which we cannot ignore and which without doubt adversely affects Puerto Rican Studies in the metropolis. c) The programs of Puerto Rican Studies—included among these is the Center of Puerto Rican Studies of the City University of New York (CUNY)—were created as a result of the profound social and political struggles of the 1960s, namely, the Black rebellion, the anti-Vietnam war movement, the university and youth counter-culture, etc. Pressured by these events, the university authorities of New York City instituted the program of open admissions as an emergency measure directed towards reaching a slightly greater ethnic balance in its university registration. This had the effect of providing access to higher education to Puerto Rican youths who were previously marginal to the education process. At the same time, it intensified the need to recruit suitable personnel for teaching Puerto Rican Studies at the university level. This meant, in practice, that traditional academic criteria for teaching had to be shelved. Consequently, people whose principal qualifications were their political and social activism, and not their knowledge or thorough study of the Puerto Rican reality, entered to form part of the departments of New York City's colleges. Even more, the attitudes of these teachers towards study, when not openly hostile, were those of indifference. One of the most bitter critics of these programs, Dr. Eduardo Seda Bonilla, points out:

> The ideals that provided the initial impetus for these programs [Puerto Rican Studies] were losing their original impulse only to fall into the hands of opportunists without university preparation, "Puerto Rican professionals" who got a whiff of what was coming and dedicated themselves to the goal of flattering students so that the students, in turn, would exercise pressure on the university administration, functioning therefore in the capacity of what the Young Lords so correctly called "poverty pimps" and not in the legitimate capacity originally formulated. The "poverty pimp" arrives in this way with the title of super-radical, super-activist, super "anti-establishment," "super-Puerto Rican," all mouth, and in reality a "super-opportunist."[16]

It is clear that Dr. Seda Bonilla is excessively caustic in his commentaries. But there is no doubt that there is a basis of truth in his warnings, however exaggerated and intemperate they seem. In fact, the prevailing attitudes among important sectors of the programs of Puerto Rican Studies turn out to be a blend of populism, anti-intellectualism and volunteerism. The very exaltation and glorification of the "lumpen-proletariat" as agents of revolutionary change, the appeal to the purely rhythmic and emotional elements as the most solidly representative of Puerto Rican culture, the tendency towards stereotyped clichés as substitutes for serious and conscientious thought, in sum, irra-tionality—through a not very well concealed contempt for intelligence and an inverted ritualistic and formalist mania which leads to intellec-tual paralysis and sterility—dressed up in revolutionary activism is what is seen more often than not in these programs.

Nevertheless, there exist tendencies in the opposite direction, particularly those which are derived from a sound understanding of the range of critical thought. As Dr. Frank Bonilla says, we are dealing with the first generation of Puerto Rican university students in the United States. Among these young people there is an enormous potential for the cultivation of critical thought, resources not yet fully tapped which could yield great fruits if they were channeled through the path of systematic studies of the Puerto Rican reality in the United States and Puerto Rico. But in order to overcome populism, irrationalism and anti-intellectualism, so foreign to critical thought, they would have to pay heed to Marx's warning to Maurice Lachatre: "There is no royal road to science, and only those who do not dread the fatiguing climb of its steep paths have a chance of gaining its luminous summits."

We sincerely believe that all of these obstacles will be overcome whenever we decide to put aside the resentments and suspicions which create a gap in communication owing to the spurious and destructive distinction between those of us who live on the Island and those who reside in the metropolis. In order to reach this goal, it is essential that those of the Island understand emphatically the process of geographic and cultural uprooting which has forced one-third of our population to emigrate. But the effort will not be less for Puerto Ricans born and raised in the United States, whose legitimate resentment toward those who had the opportunity to remain on the Island often clouds their perspective with respect to us "of the Island." We have too much to learn from one another in these unfortunate moments, for us to weaken ourselves in internecine fights that only lead to self-destruction.

The second important question from a cultural perspective are the programs of bilingual education created under the Law of Bilingual Education passed in 1965 by the United States Congress. The law itself is very important from an ideological point of view, since it reflects, on the one hand, a raising of consciousness of the established system with respect to the diverse "ethnics" that live within the U.S. territory, and on the other hand, a strategy to fight against the problem of cultural diversity without sacrificing in the long run the "sacred" principle of cultural assimilation. Because of its implications, the Law of Bilingual Education deserves to be quoted here, especially Title VII which sets up the following:

a) Acknowledging

1. That there are large numbers of children whose ability to speak English is limited;
2. That many of these children have a cultural heritage that differs from that of English-speaking people;
3. That one of the principal means for a child's learning is through the use of his language and cultural heritage;
4. That, therefore, large numbers of children with a limited ability to speak English have educational needs that can be met through the use of methods and techniques of bilingual education; and
5. That, in addition, children of limited ability in the use of the English language are benefited through the fullest utilization of multiple linguistic and cultural resources.

The United States Congress declares that it is the policy of the United States, in seeking to establish equal educational opportunities for all children, a) to encourage the establishment and operation when appropriate of educational programs that utilize bilingual practices, techniques, methods, etc.; b) to provide financial aid for this goal to local and state educational authorities so that they develop and carry out these programs in elementary and secondary schools, including pre-school level activities designed to serve the educational needs of these children; and to demonstrate effective and human ways of providing instruction that will permit children of limited English ability the use of their vernacular tongue as well as teach them the competent use of the English language.

As can be observed, the use of the vernacular—whether it be Chinese or Spanish—is conceived as a necessary step for the eventual command of the English language. This is recognition of an undeniable reality; that there are hundreds of thousands of children in the United States whose language is not English. But at the same time, they seek to make a virtue of this need, and they make it a convenient resource that allows for the temporary resolution of the problem at least, without losing sight of their long-range goal, which is nothing but cultural assimilation, that is, the North Americanization of all nationalities who reside on U.S. soil.[17]

Nevertheless, bilingual problems should not be considered in a purely negative light. On the contrary, these problems have many positive aspects, namely the acknowledgment, no matter how reluctant, of the U.S. government that there exists a cultural reality that resists to the utmost the traditional outlines for assimilation, and the fact that in spite of objectives in the opposite direction, education in the vernacular is often more, much more, than the simple change of language. It is the communication of a whole complex network of meanings that leaves its indelible imprint on the cultural formation of the Spanish-speaking child.

Nor should we deceive ourselves by believing that these programs constitute the panacea for the Puerto Rican cultural question in the United States or in Puerto Rico (where they have had to institute bilingual programs, but the other way around, given the percentage of children who return from the United States and do not know Spanish).

The problem, like all social problems, is of a dialectical nature and ought to be analyzed as such. Both the programs of Puerto Rican Studies and those of bilingual education are products of a struggle unleashed not only by that part of our people who live in the United States, but by all the other peoples who have been forced to emigrate to the great capitalist metropolis, coming from Asia, Africa or Latin America. The concessions of the regime are not gifts. They have been fought for and won. Amidst the gaps and contradictions created by the capitalist system, in its attempt to neutralize and assimilate our people, the importance of cultural affirmation stands out, not as a mere academic exercise, but as a manifestation of culture as a battlefield of national and class struggle, as a fortification of resistance, a dimension of unquestionable profundity.

Mother Borinquen calls me
This country is not mine
Borinquen is pure flame
And here I am freezing to death.
                                    POPULAR SONG

7

THOSE WHO RETURN

In his novel *Ardiente suelo, fría estación,* the Puerto Rican writer Pedro
Juan Soto has written about the odyssey of a young Puerto Rican who
searches for his identity among the opposite poles of New York and San
Juan. The principal character of the work lives "in the air"—literally
and metaphorically—between Puerto Rico and New York City. Actually, this experience is not a foreign one for an ever-growing number of
Puerto Ricans. The flow of passengers from the Island to the metropolis, and the flow back to the Island, is a daily fact that can be seen every
day in the waiting rooms of airports. In his study on the subject of the
return of Puerto Rican emigrants, to which we will also refer later, Dr.
Hernández Alvarez tells us:

> At least one out of every three persons born in Puerto Rico has experienced
> living in the United States at some time in his life. The other two have known
> migration in an indirect way by visiting the mainland and or as a conse-
> quence of the departure of relatives, friends, and acquaintances. Most
> genuine migrants have remained in the United States, although an ever-
> increasing number have returned to Puerto Rico. Since the mid-1950s the
> reverse flow has become an important aspect of Puerto Rican life. Today, at
> least 145,000 of the Island's inhabitants are returning migrants.

Given that reality, it should not surprise us if the colonialist
panaceas fall short of or never hit the target. The only way of sustaining
the economy seems to be ever-growing doses of aid from the U.S.
Federal Government. This practice, far from resolving the problems of
unemployment and pauperism, makes them even more desperate.
The future of Puerto Ricans who return is therefore not dis-

tinguished in a perceptible way from the future of those who leave. To escape from capitalism only to fall into colonial-capitalism, or to escape from the latter to fall into the former, is simply and frankly to move one's geographic position within the same area of exploitation.

The economy of the future socialist republic of Puerto Rico ought to be structured in such a way that all Puerto Ricans who desire to return to the homeland can do so without fear of being reduced to indigence. The rehabilitation and restructuring of agriculture, the social and rational planning of our natural resources, the optimal utilization of a labor force fully integrated into the productive process; all these means should put an end to the sad exodus marked by a return empty of all hope.

Given the present economic crisis through which capitalism is passing, it can be expected that the tendency toward the migratory return will become stronger and stronger. The relocation and placing of these compatriots within a broken and battered colonial economy will pose problems even more serious than those that presently confront the colonial government of Puerto Rico.

The problem of the reintegration of Puerto Ricans who return to the heart of Puerto Rican society is part of the global problem of the entire capitalist-colonialist economy. This reintegration cannot take place, moreover, without radically modifying the orientation which up until now has guided the thought and action of the principal colonialist parties. More comprehensively still, the problems of the migratory flow in and out, not only of Puerto Ricans, but of however many suffer from the exploitation consubstantive to the capitalist mode of production, will be able to be remedied only when this system has been definitively abolished by the world proletariat.

The flow in and out of the Island is of great importance for the study of the Puerto Rican national reality. It would be interesting, moreover, to study the phenomenon of the passage itself between the colony and the metropolis: what this passage reveals about the social composition of the travelers, the ties they break or keep with the Island and the metropolis, the cultural features which flourish in the farewell rituals which precede the air crossing of the Atlantic, etc. These are fascinating themes which perhaps we will approach on another occasion.

For now, what interests us is the fact that among Puerto Ricans who emigrate to the United States, there is a growing number who

return to Puerto Rico after having lived on the continent for a considerable extent of time. Some want to see this return as an unqualified
romantic evocation of a "return to the roots," an attempt to return to
the old communities, to the idyllic Puerto Rican life, seen as a principally agrarian and patriarchal society. This tendency toward the
idealization of an agrarian past has been very pronounced among
prominent sectors of the *criollo* literary elite, especially among those
with strong Luddite inclinations, for whom the return to nature is a
kind of regenerative force, given the dissolving and alienating tendencies of urbanism and industrialization.[1] Others think they see in this
process a concrete illustration that our compatriots have realized the
dream of prosperity offered by "the promised land" of the North, and
that this is why they return, as victorious bearers of good news. Lastly,
there are those who see in this reverse exodus the return of the defeated
and displaced, the ominous signal that emigration as "escape valve" is
progressively losing the steam that used to drive it.

   Putting aside for the moment the literary theses, we are confronted
with a socio-economic fact of capital importance. I am referring to the
fact that the migratory flow between Puerto Rico and the United States
shows a pronounced tendency to grow or diminish in concordance with
the economic cycles characteristic of the capitalist system. That is, in
those moments characterized by a rapid accumulation of capital in the
metropolis, the Puerto Rican working masses are attracted to the
capitalist center, whereas in periods of economic recession or depression, an inverse tendency takes place: the flow of migrants to the United
States diminishes and the tendency towards the return of those who are
repelled by the U.S. job market is intensified. Thus, for example, a
recent study by the Emigration Division of the Department of Labor of
the "Free Associated State of Puerto Rico" indicates that 21,000 Puerto
Ricans returned to the Island between 1970 and 1974. The question has
worried not a few ideologues, especially those who see in the emigration
"with no return" the key to the entire economic growth of Puerto Rico.
For these ideologues, the return of *Boricuan* workers worries them
more than their continual exodus to the United States.

   But let us return to the problem that concerns us by placing the first
question: *who* is returning and *why?* We believe that this question
requires a more detailed answer than the one we just offered. In the
second place, we should ask ourselves what the consequences of
returning are for those who have done so.

Fortunately, we have at hand two studies which help to shed light on these questions. There is, first, the important study by Dr. José Hernández Alvarez, *Return Migration to Puerto Rico,* and, second, a recent study by Professors Celia Fernández de Cintrón and Pedro Vales Hernández, published in 1974 by the Centro de Investigaciones Sociales of the University of Puerto Rico, also under the title, *Return Migration to Puerto Rico.* Of both studies, the most complete and systematic is that of Dr. Hernández Alvarez, since he has placed the problem within a global context. Nevertheless, this study is to a great degree a product of the experiences of the 1950s and 1960s, which is why it requires that we see it through a critical prism in light of the experiences of the 1970s.

Dr. Hernández Alvarez says, referring to those who return to Puerto Rico from the metropolis:

> Within the present context of Puerto Rico as a developing country, return migrants generally represent a middle-class element, bordering on the Island's educational, occupational, and financial elite. Many have taken advantage of opportunities becoming available as a result of modernization, resuming life in Puerto Rico under favorable circumstances—as professionals, white-collar workers, and highly skilled technicians.[2]

According to Hernández Alvarez's description, Puerto Rican migrants who return to Puerto Rico are mostly those who have "progressed," that is, those who have succeeded in climbing the social ladder, and who now return to the Island in an advantageous position. It will be difficult to accept this thesis without further questioning. The same author (writing in 1967), tells us that there are 145,000 people that could be considered migrants in the sense already described. We should ask, first, if such a considerable sector is for the most part classified under the category of the "middle layers." In the second place, we should ask ourselves if the present situation offers support to Dr. Hernández Alvarez's thesis, now that the crisis of the capitalist system has forced the return of thousands of Puerto Ricans who could not under any circumstance be classified as belonging to the middle class. Dr. Hernández Alvarez himself tells us that:

> At the middle of the 1960s, the large group of emigrants remaining on the mainland are mainly oriented toward the same economic activities which attracted them a decade or more ago. Although earning substantially more than most people in the homeland, they are experiencing industrial displacement resulting from the mechanization and automation of the routine and repetitive tasks they are accustomed to perform. Also caught by the "leveling

up" of educational requirements for employment, as well as difficulties related to language and ethnic identity, the Puerto Ricans in the United States are encountering serious difficulties in finding and keeping jobs.[3]

In other words, the displacement of the Puerto Rican work force in the United States is throwing out into the streets *Boricuan* workers in growing numbers. This displacement, which we already saw taking place in the 1960s, has been dramatically intensified in the 1970s. This ought to be reason enough to review Dr. Hernández Alvarez's generalizations critically since, short of completely discarding his original thesis on the social position of the Puerto Rican emigrants who return, who cannot do less than indicate how and in what way the displaced and unemployed are returning by the thousands to Puerto Rico. This is precisely one of the great fears repeatedly expressed by the ideologues who see emigration as an "escape valve." They regard with profound apprehension this flow to Puerto Rico, which seems to hurl to the ground one of the cornerstones of their overly praised "economic growth."

In any case, the displacement lashes out with singular force at Puerto Rican workers, at Afro-Americans, Chicanos, etc.; that is, at all those groups classified as "non-whites" within U.S. society. The following observation by Baran and Sweezy on Afro-Americans is even more valid when applied to Puerto Ricans:

> Since 1950, on the other hand, with unskilled jobs disappearing at a fantastic rate, Negroes not qualified for other kinds of work found themselves increasingly excluded from employment altogether. Hence the rise of the Negro unemployment rate to more than double the white rate by the early 1960s. Negroes, in other words, being the least qualified workers are disproportionately hard hit as unskilled jobs (and, to an increasing extent, semi-skilled jobs) are eliminated by mechanization, automation, and cybernation.[4]

Nevertheless, we are dealing with something more than a simple technological displacement: we are confronted rather with a tendency peculiar to capitalism in its monopoly stage, and with what Harry Braverman describes succinctly for us in the following way:

> . . . it [the degradation of work in the twentieth century] consists in the narrowing of the base of productive labor upon which the economy rests, to the point where an ever smaller portion of society labors to maintain all of it, while the remainder is drafted, at lower rates of pay and even more demeaning conditions of labor, into the productive economy of capitalism. And finally, it consists in the misery of unemployment and outright pauper-

ization, which are aspects of the reserve army of labor created by capital more or less automatically in its accumulation process.[5]

The question, however, should not remain at the abstract level. The most recent study on Puerto Ricans in the United States (Wagenheim) confirms this tendency and agrees with Dr. Hernández Alvarez's predictions, as well as with the perceptive observations of Baran, Sweezy and Braverman. In this study, it is indicated that:

> More and more old factories that employ large numbers of minority workers are shutting down and in some cases relocating at suburban sites . . .

> It is no surprise, then, that between 1950 and 1971, almost all of New York City's job growth was in service-producing industries such as transportation, public utilities, trade, finance, and government.

The author goes on to conclude with the following note:

> Thus, unless there is a radical improvement in the education and training of Puerto Ricans, unless there is migration to areas where jobs exist, unless the American economy heats up and provides jobs for the many poor, semi-skilled or unskilled persons who are now marginal to the society, unless the federal government finally delivers the guaranteed family income plan that has so long been debated, it appears that Puerto Ricans and all groups who now inhabit the inner cities will face a grim struggle for economic survival in the coming decade.[6]

Unless! "Unless" structural changes are made in the capitalist economy, there will of course be no solution to the problems enumerated by Wagenheim. But this is another problem. What is important to us at this time is to stress the fact that return emigration to the Island does not result from simple individual decisions based on fortuitous circumstances, but rather is a part of a broader and more embracing social process which takes place independently of the will of those who suffer it. This is not a sociohistoric fact separate from that of those who are forced to emigrate to the United States; rather it forms a part of the whole dynamic of the Island as a supplier of a cheap and abundant labor force. Even more, we are dealing with the entire Caribbean as a supply area of a willing labor force reserve for U.S. capitalism. Capital moves where it can increase the process of accumulation and withdraws from those areas where this process shows signs of diminishing. This process takes place in the metropolis itself, as we have had occasion to see. Therefore, the labor force of Puerto Ricans is attracted or discarded, absorbed or repelled, in accordance with the needs of the capitalist system itself. The same thing happens with the work force from Jamaica, the Dominican Republic, Haiti, etc. We are emphasizing the global character of the problem and not its particular manifestations.

From that point of view, it is worthwhile to point out that the present rulers of the "Free Associated State" are now claiming to have become jealous guardians of the Puerto Ricans' right to work, in the face of the competition from workers from the rest of the Caribbean. That is why they have taken up a campaign against "illegal immigrants," especially Dominicans, who supposedly are taking away jobs from Puerto Rican workers, a campaign they have never thought of taking up against Cuban exiles, who today exceed 50,000 on our Island. Even more, the Secretary of Labor, Dr. Luis F. Silva Recio, has begun a crusade against some 5,000 Jamaicans who have gone to the eastern United States to harvest apples. According to the Secretary of Labor, these jobs should be awarded with preference to Puerto Ricans, since they are "citizens of the United States." It is curious that Dr. Silva Recio has concluded that having an excess work force produces a depressing effect on salaries. Curious, because it would seem as if he, like Moliere's legendary character, had been speaking prose (that is, Marxism) all his life without even knowing it. (See *The San Juan Star*, July 17, 1975, p. 8.)

Let us pass now to the subject of the return of the emigrants to their homeland.

In the first place, those who return to the Island from the United States today encounter an ever bleaker panorama with respect to the chances of finding jobs. Welfare and unemployment benefits are reduced much more on the Island than they are in the metropolis. None of these two factors seems to have been of a dissuasive character for the increase in the flow of those who return. In any case, we have to understand a fact of great significance: the situation of those who return is not much better than that of those who remain in the United States.

Naturally, the return of these compatriots tends to aggravate the unemployment problem in Puerto Rico, which is why the reactionary press and the neo-Malthusian ideologues have begun to emit the well-known laments with respect to the "population explosion" and its ill-fated consequences, etc. They are arguments which we have already examined and which we will not repeat here. Suffice it to indicate, that for these ideologues there is no greater danger for the political stability of Puerto Rico than the return of the former emigrants to their native land, irrefutable evidence of their political immorality.

In the second place, those who return confront serious problems of adjustment in the cultural field. This is singularly applicable in the cases of those Puerto Ricans born in the United States after World War II. Here we encounter a problem which is the reverse of the one we mentioned before, when we spoke about bilingual programs in New York City. Now we are not dealing with teaching Puerto Rican children in Spanish because they do not know English, but with teaching Puerto Rican children in English because they do not know Spanish.

Of course, a problem of a generational nature has existed throughout this entire process. Nevertheless, it is imperative to note that Puerto Rico's public schools confront a very acute problem. Puerto Rican children who come from the metropolis and who do not know Spanish suffer all the hardships of the lack of communication, rejection and culture shock. As a matter of fact, most of them are forced to live in a kind of cultural no-man's land. This tends to increase their feelings of insecurity and it makes their identity as Puerto Ricans more problematic.

Dr. Israel Ramos Perea, in his doctoral dissertation on the adjustment to school of children who are returned migrants to Puerto Rico, tells us:

> . . . it has been reported that many students wanted to return to the United States . . . "they don't fit in here . . . ," "the English-speaking students generally hang out together" or because "their Spanish-speaking friends generally corrected their bad Spanish, but only after they had had a big laugh." (A survey carried out in 1966–1967 of 2,470 return migrant children showed that 50.7% were having difficulties with Spanish.) Another study of 11,079 return migrant children showed that their greatest difficulty was based on reading, writing, understanding and speaking Spanish.[7]

The rejection of those who have come to be called *New Yorricans* should be understood in all its cultural and social dimensions, in all that it represents for our society.* It is one more gap extended between Puerto Ricans "from here" and "from over there." Unfortunately, these differences are revived by those groups or individuals interested in creating artificial divisions within Puerto Rican society. The Department of Public Instruction has treated the problem as one that can be resolved by assigning specialized teachers to the task of teaching

---

*The problem was illustrated dramatically in a recent article by David Vidal under the title, "The Loneliness of the Returning Newyorican," *Sunday San Juan Star,* October 5, 1975.

English where there are great concentrations of returned migrant children. The false thesis of the bilingualism of Puerto Ricans is accepted without even questioning it. All this tends to aggravate the confusion of the Puerto Rican child and to sharpen his identity problems. Far from freeing the Puerto Rican child from the colonialist syndromes, public education in Puerto Rico emphasizes even more the vices of colonialism. The net result of all this is the perpetration of pedagogical practices whose goals are submission and authoritarianism.

In the third place, we must point out that the political consequences of the flow of people between the colony and the metropolis are very profound and significant. The continual traffic between Puerto Rico and the United States gives Puerto Ricans an extraordinary mobility at the same time as it allows them to compare their experiences in contexts dissimilar geographically but similar socially and economically. The condition of the working or unemployed *Boricuan* in the United States is not fundamentally different than that of his or her homonym in Puerto Rico. Even more, we can say that the condition of the Puerto Rican worker in Puerto Rico or in the United States is not essentially different from that of the non-white proletariat of the capitalist countries of the center, insofar as these countries are seen forced to import growing quantities of a labor force from colonial and neocolonial countries. As Samir Amin tells us:

> Moreover, the idea that the proletariat at the center is a privileged group, and thus necessarily in alliance with its own bourgeoisie in exploiting the Third World, is only a simplification of the real position. True, with equal productivity, the proletariat at the center averages higher rewards than the workers in the periphery. But in order to fight against the law of the tendency for the rate of profit to fall at the center, capital imports labor from the periphery, which it pays at a lower rate (and assigns the least attractive kinds of work) and which it also uses to bring down wages in the metropolitan labor market. This importing of labor has assumed considerable dimensions: in Western Europe and in North America the increase in immigration from the periphery has increased annually since 1960 by a percentage ranging from 0.7 percent to 1.9 percent, depending on the countries and the years—in other words, at levels that are, on the average, much higher than the rates of growth of the national labor force; this contribution of labor power of immigrant origin also constitutes a hidden transfer of value from the periphery to the center, since the periphery has borne the cost of education and training this labor power.[8]

The dimension on a world scale of this problem increases the revolutionary potential of the Puerto Rican proletariat, whether in the United States or in Puerto Rico. When seen in this light, we better understand the reason for the Puerto Rican bourgeoisie's fear of the return of the emigrants to the Island. Its class instincts tell it that there is a potential danger in this return to the homeland by great human contingents that "have nothing to lose" by such a change.

This leads us to some final thoughts about the subject that concerns us in this chapter. Because the truth is that we would not want to conclude without outlining some hasty and perhaps formal reflections on what some people have come to call *New Yorricans*.[9]

The dimension of the problem can be felt in the figures compiled by the Center of Demographic Studies of the School of Medicine of the University of Puerto Rico, which Dr. José Luis Vásquez Calzada directs. According to Dr. Vásquez Calzada, there were in 1970, 128,000 children of migrants in Puerto Rico, of whom approximately 85,000 (that is to say, 70 percent) were under fifteen years of age. As the reader will observe, we are talking about Puerto Ricans *not born* in Puerto Rico. This implies that the immense majority of them do not know how to speak Spanish, or they speak it with great difficulty. Most of these compatriots have settled in urban areas such as Santa Juanita in Bayamon, Levittown in Toa Baja and Villa Carolina in Carolina. The problems of adjustment to Puerto Rican society, especially among the youngest, sharpen the problems of identity and lead to considerable frictions with Puerto Ricans "from here." We pointed this out earlier but we ought to dig deeper into the problem.

In the first place, the presence of these Puerto Ricans who have arrived in Puerto Rico and who do not know Spanish has engendered chauvinism and social and racial prejudice among considerable sectors of the Puerto Rican population, especially in the middle layers. It is truly shocking that those who most stridently preach their philo-Yankeeism are at the same time those who reject some people because they speak in English. Why? Because they often wear "Afros" or behave in a "different" way than those here on the Island? There is no doubt that at the bottom of the question throbs an economic problem: in a country of 40 percent unemployment, everyone who returns potentially threatens the jobs of those whose job security is precarious. Nor should we disregard the tendentious and pernicious campaign against those who return, a campaign waged through the mass media of the country. But there is more. There is what Franz Fanon refers to as the "inferiorization" of the colonized and their tendency toward self-violence, toward the destruction of their own family and toward self-destruction.[10]

The most characteristic thing about the colonial relationship between Puerto Rico and the United States, when seen from the cultural perspective, has been its ambiguity. We Puerto Ricans are and are not North Americans, we are and are not Latin Americans. The definition in each case takes place necessarily within the framework imposed by the system in force. In any case, we Puerto Ricans find ourselves in an anomalous condition before other peoples of Spanish America. Everyone of us who has traveled to the southern hemisphere knows that we are received with suspicion when not with open indifference. Since most of those who travel are people from the Puerto Rican petty bourgeoisie or high bourgeoisie—they are consequently profoundly imbued with the colonialist world-view—and as compensation, they seek to protect themselves with their U.S. citizenship, which presumedly places them on the side of the masters. Nevertheless, people are not always taken in by this, and rejection is not postponed for long.

These attitudes of rejection, of course, take place to the greatest degree in the United States. There, racism permeates all social relations. After a time in the metropolis, the average Puerto Rican realizes that there are North Americans who do not like him. A great disillusionment. The fact of prejudice becomes more acute especially among Puerto Ricans who live in the United States. That is why many Puerto Rican youths, born there, responding to an idealized vision of Puerto Rico, want to find the Island so as to find themselves. The illusionary bubble bursts rapidly: Puerto Rico is not the bucolic place that Rafael Hernández describes in his *Lamento Borincano*,* nor do its inhabitants display that proverbial hospitality of which so much is said.

But once this return is permanent, the Puerto Rican born in the United States discovers that he is the target of the hostility of those of the Island. They call him *New Yorrican* "because he hasn't learned Spanish," "because he doesn't dress like everyone else," etc. A curious reaction. The so-called *New Yorrican* becomes a scapegoat, the victim of a national chauvinism strange in a people who have not been known for their national fervor. The reaction is stronger and more virulent among the middle strata who see the returnees as the incarnation of all

*Probably Puerto Rico's most popular national song.

the evils that afflict our land. Because those who have come to be called *New Yorricans* are the reminder—in flesh and blood—for those who believed that they could give up one-third of our population as a necessary means so that those of us who did not have to emigrate could enjoy a high standard of living.

The ironies of history. The *Boricuan* intermediary bourgeoisie and the petty bourgeoisie thought that their problems of economic development were to have been resolved with the emigratory "escape valve." But they did not count on the fact that those who had to leave would return someday, bringing with them an entire generation of Puerto Ricans as evidence of the bitter fruits which are products of the "Free Associated State." In their desperation, they seek and find a group of Puerto Ricans whom they can brand as "inferior," or "not Puerto Rican." Reality, however, takes charge and balances the picture. The incorrectly labeled *New Yorricans* are as Puerto Rican as any of us; this land belongs to them as much or more than to those who have handed it over palm tree by palm tree to the colonizers of our people. This is not the time to wash our hands of this question, but rather to assume the historic responsibilities and welcome as our own those who return to the HOMELAND.

Philosophers have only interpreted the world, in various ways; the point however is to change it.

KARL MARX

FINAL OBSERVATIONS

If this book has succeeded in firmly establishing that Puerto Rican emigration to the United States has been an integral part of the entire strategy of the development—we should say, to be more precise, the "anti-development"—of Puerto Rico during the last three decades, it will have fulfilled its objective. Puerto Rican emigration has not been the product of simple fortuitous and disconnected events, but rather has been the result of some government decisions whose anti-national character is overwhelmingly evident. The leaders of the colonial parties of Puerto Rico have all been equal accomplices in this crime of treason perpetrated against the Puerto Rican working class.

If this essay has succeeded in communicating to the reader that Puerto Rican emigration is part of a global phenomenon within the capitalist mode of production, it will have also fulfilled its objective. The exploitation suffered by the Puerto Rican emigrant can be compared to that of the Algerian or Jamaican. The problem of emigration is therefore one of international character and not limited to the national. It is necessary that we Puerto Ricans break out of the tight circle to which imperialism together with the native colonialists have condemned us.

But this work is something more than a critical focus on Puerto Rican emigration. What has been on trial here, more than anything else, has been the strategy of dependent development whose most worn out expression has been "Fomento Económico." This strategy of economic development is found today to be totally bankrupt. Puerto Rico finds itself subjected to the worst economic crisis in its history. Today the "showcase" does not have anything to show the world except its hand perennially extended toward Washington. The ineffable "developmentist" Teodoro Moscoso has carried our people to the very doors of indigence, which is why our economy can only be kept afloat by massive injections of U.S. aid. The program of industrial incentives begun in 1947 has failed disgracefully while Mr. Moscoso continues his delirium about possibly establishing a "super port," copper mine exploitation, and so on.

Let it be clear that we are not the ones who have documented the failure of "Fomento." This has been predicted and confirmed for many years by the very economists at the service of colonialism. But now there is even more. The Governor of the "Free Associated State," Rafael Hernández Colón, solicited a study on the state of the economy of Puerto Rico from a group of prominent U.S. economists. This study, known popularly as the "Tobin Report" (one of its members was Dr. James Tobin of the Department of Economics at Yale University), has diagnosed the disastrous state of our economy and has severely indicted the supposed social benefits of the program of "Fomento."[1]

The Tobin Report proposes as solutions greater austerity in salaries, that is, that the working class should pay for the errors committed, and a policy of "import substitutions" to reduce our dependence on the exterior. All this, naturally, is to be carried out without fundamentally changing the colonial structures in Puerto Rico. This is the reason the Tobin Report only offers, in the long run, one more palliative for the battered Puerto Rican economy.

In the face of this colonialist alternative, we propose independence and true socialism, the alternative that represents a radical transformation of the Puerto Rican economy and solidifies the power of the Puerto Rican working class as the leading class of our homeland. We are echoing, thereby, the 19th century thesis of Marx on Feuerbach: "The philosphers have only interpreted the world, in various ways; the point however is to *change* it."

APPENDIX

TABLE 1.

PUERTO RICANS IN THE UNITED STATES, 1910-1974

	Total	Percentage Increase	Percentage of Total in N.Y.C.	Born in P.R.	Born in U.S.A.
1910	1,513	—	36.6	1,513	—
1920	11,811	680.6	62.3	11,811	—
1930	52,774	346.8	—	52,774	—
1940	69,967	32.6	87.8	69,967	—
1950	301,375	330.7	81.6	226,110	75,265
1960	887,662	194.5	69.0	615,384	272,278
1970	1,429,396	61.0	58.8	783,358	646,038
1974	1,548,000	—	—	—	—

SOURCES: *1960 Census of Population,* "Puerto Ricans in the United States," PC(2) ID, Table A, p. viii, and *1970 Census of Population,* "Persons of Spanish Ancestry," PC (S1)-30, February 1973, Table I, p. I. "Persons of Spanish Origin in the United States; March 1974," Series P-20, no. 267, July 1974.

TABLE 2.

PUERTO RICANS IN THE UNITED STATES AND IN PUERTO RICO, 1960-1970

	1960	1970
In Puerto Rico	2,349,540	2,712,033
Born in Puerto Rico	2,287,200	2,432,828
Born in the United States of Puerto Rican parentage	49,092	106,602
In Continental U.S.A.	887,662	1,429,396
Born in Puerto Rico	615,384	783,358
Born in the United States of Puerto Rican parentage	272,278	646,038

SOURCE: *1970 Census of Population,* "Puerto Ricans in the United States," PC(2) IE, Table I, p. xi.

TABLE 3.

STATES WHERE PUERTO RICANS RESIDED, 1960-1970

	1960	1970		1960	1970
Alabama	663	1,028	Montana	53	341
Alaska	562	534	Nebraska	333	389
Arizona	1,008	1,047	Nevada	179	674
Arkansas	207	139	New Hampshire	212	425
California	28,108	50,917	New Jersey	55,351	138,896
Colorado	844	1,707	New Mexico	433	411
Connecticut	15,247	37,609	New York	642,622	916,825
Delaware	773	2,486	North		
District of			Carolina	1,866	2,482
Columbia	1,373	1,046	North Dakota	68	88
Florida	19,535	28,166	Ohio	13,940	20,272
Georgia	2,334	3,615	Oklahoma	1,398	1,124
Hawaii	4,289	9,300	Oregon	233	522
Idaho	60	232	Pennsylvania	21,206	44,263
Illinois	36,081	87,509	Rhode Island	447	981
Indiana	7,218	9,269	South		
Iowa	226	428	Carolina	1,114	2,096
Kansas	1,136	683	South Dakota	124	44
Kentucky	1,376	860	Tennessee	499	1,127
Louisiana	1,935	2,430	Texas	6,050	6,334
Maine	403	426	Utah	473	739
Maryland	3,229	6,262	Vermont	108	215
Massachusetts	5,217	23,332	Virginia	2,971	4,098
Michigan	3,806	6,202	Washington	1,739	1,845
Minnesota	387	490	West Virginia	252	73
Mississippi	301	478	Wisconsin	3,574	7,248
Missouri	940	1,801	Wyoming	50	56

SOURCES: *1960 Census of the Population,* "Puerto Ricans in the United States," PC(2) 1D, Table 15, pp. 103–104; *1970 Census of the Population,* "Persons of Spanish Origin," PC (SI)-30, February 1973, Table 1, p. 1.

TABLE 4.

YEARS OF SCHOOL COMPLETED BY PUERTO RICANS IN THE U.S.A. AND IN PUERTO RICO COMPARED WITH SCHOOL YEARS COMPLETED BY TOTAL U.S. POPULATION, 1970

	Total	IN THE UNITED STATES		IN PUERTO RICO	
		Born in Puerto Rico	Born in the U.S.A.	Born in Puerto Rico	Born in the U.S.A.
Population 25 years and older	567,462	509,456	58,006		
Percentage with less than 5 completed school years	23.7	20.5	45.6	37.8	5.0
Percentage with 4 years of high school	23.0			27.0	52.3
Percentage with 4 years of university	2.2	1.9	5.4	6.0	10.0
Median School years completed	8.6	8.4	11.5	6.9	12.1

SOURCES: *1970 Census of the Population*, "Puerto Ricans in the United States," PC(2)-IE, Table 4, p. 34; "General Social and Economic Characteristics, Puerto Rico," PC(1) 53 P.R. Table 45, pp. 53–197; *1970 Census of the Population*, "General Social and Economic Characteristics, Summary of the United States," PC(1) C1, Table 75, pp. 1–368.

TABLE 5.

ANNUAL INCOME OF FAMILIES OF SPANISH ORIGIN

	TOTAL U.S.A.	FAMILIES OF SPANISH ORIGIN			
		Total*	Mexicans	Puerto Ricans	Cubans
Number of families	53,296,000	2,057,000	1,100,000	363,000	170,000
Percentage	100.0	100.0	100.0	100.0	100.0
Income Range					
Less than $3 000	8.3	13.8	14.9	16.9	7.9
$3 000 - 3 999	4.8	8.2	9.2	11.0	3.2
$4 000 - 4 999	5.4	8.4	7.1	10.6	11.3
$5 000 - 5 999	5.7	8.1	8.3	10.2	8.0
$6 000 - 6 999	5.5	7.2	7.0	7.7	3.5
$7 000 - 7 999	6.2	8.0	7.1	12.8	7.6
$8 000 - 9 999	12.3	13.8	15.1	9.9	11.8
$10 000 - 11 999	12.5	11.9	11.8	10.6	15.1
$12 000 - 14 999	14.4	10.4	10.2	5.1	10.2
$15 000 - 24 999	19.5	9.5	8.6	4.5	20.6
$25 000 or more	5.3	0.9	0.5	0.8	0.8
Average family income	$10,285	$7,548	$7,486	$6,185	$9,371

SOURCE: Office of the Census of the United States, report of the present population, Series P–20; the family figures are for March 1972.   *Includes other people of Spanish origin

TABLE 6.

PUERTO RICAN MIGRATION, 1960-1974

	Net Migration from Puerto Rico to the Continental U.S.A.*	Net Migration to Puerto Rico from Foreign Countries and U.S. Virgin Is.**
1960	19,101	2,803
1961	— 230	1,562
1962	11,398	— 266
1963	3,206	8,685
1964	4,200	2,830
1965	27,026	10,348
1966	39,053	10,891
1967	46,644	16,315
1968	—14,249	9,604
1969	66,674	23,614
1970	20,715	21,869
1971	4,951	17,861
1972	—34,015	— 359
1973	—20,948	13,433
1974	9,535	27,913

SOURCE: Planning Board of the ELA of Puerto Rico. Migration is calculated comparing arrivals and departures in the airports of Puerto Rico.

*A negative sign (- -) indicates migration from the Continental United States to Puerto Rico.
**A negative sign (—) indicates migration from Puerto Rico to foreign countries and to the Virgin Islands (U.S.A.).

TABLE 7.

STATES WITH LARGE PUERTO RICAN POPULATIONS, 1960-1970

	1960	1970
California	28,108	50,917
Connecticut	15,247	37,609
Florida	19,535	28,166
Georgia	2,334	3,615
Hawaii	4,289	9,300
Illinois	36,081	87,509
Indiana	7,218	9,269
Maryland	3,229	6,262
Massachusetts	5,217	23,332
Michigan	3,806	6,202
New Jersey	55,351	138,896
New York	642,622	916,325
Ohio	13,940	20,272
Pennsylvania	21,206	44,263
Texas	6,050	6,334
Virginia	2,971	4,098
Wisconsin	3,574	7,248

SOURCES: *1960 Census of the Population,* "Puerto Ricans in the United States," PC(2) 1K, Table 15, pp. 103-104; and *Census of the United States,* "Persons of Spanish Ancestry," PC(S1)-30, February 1973, Table 1, p. 1.

TABLE 8.

Cities of the United States with 5,000 or More Puerto Ricans, 1960-1970

	1960	1970
New York, N.Y.	612,574	887,119
Chicago, Illinois	32,371	86,277
Philadelphia, Pa.	14,424	40,930
Newark, N.J.	9,698	27,009
Los Angeles, Cal.	6,424	20,500
Miami, Florida	6,547	18,918
Jersey City, N.J.	7,427	19,362
San Francisco, Cal.	—	13,511
Paterson, N.J.	5,123	13,378
Hoboken, N.J.	5,313	10,047
Bridgeport, Conn.	5,084	9,618
Hartford, Conn.	—	8,278
Cleveland, Ohio	—	8,135
Boston, Mass.	—	7,747
Washington, D.C.	—	6,732
Passaic, N.J.	—	6,609
Honolulu, Hawaii	—	6,428
Buffalo, N.Y.	—	6,090
Rochester, N.Y.	—	5,916
Milwaukee, Wis.	—	5,889
Lorain, Ohio	—	5,601
Gary, Indiana	—	5,228

Sources: *1960 Census of the United States,* "Puerto Ricans in the United States," PC(2) 1D, Table 15, p. 103; and *1970 Census of the United States,* "Persons of Spanish Ancestry," PC(S1)-30, February 1973, Table 2, pp. 2-8.

138

TABLE 9.

Puerto Ricans in Puerto Rico and in Continental United States, 1910-1974

		Total	Percentage of Yearly Increase	Born in Puerto Rico	Born in United States
In Puerto Rico					
	1910	1,118,012	—	—	—
	1920	1,299,809	16.3	—	—
	1930	1,543,913	18.8	—	—
	1940	1,869,255	21.1	—	—
	1950	2,210,703	18.3	—	—
	1960	2,349,544	6.3	2,287,200	49,092
	1970	2,712,033	15.4	2,432,828	106,602
	1974	2,951,600	—	—	—
In Continental United States					
	1910	1,513	—	—	—
	1920	11,811	680.6	—	—
	1930	52,774	346.8	—	—
	1940	69,967	32.6	—	—
	1950	301,375	330.7	226,110	75,265
	1960	887,662	194.5	615,384	272,278
	1970	1,429,396	61.0	783,358	646,038
	1974	1,458,000	—	—	—

Sources: *1970 Census of the United States,* "Number of inhabitants, Puerto Rico." PC(1)-A53. P.R. Table 1, pp. 53–59. *1960 Census of the United States,* "Puerto Ricans in the United States." PC(2) 1D, Table A, p. viii. *1970 Census of the United States,* "Persons of Spanish Ancestry," PC(S1)-30, February 1973, Table 1, p. 1.

Note: The reports of the census from 1910 to 1940 do not differentiate between Puerto Ricans born on the Island and those born on the continent. Moreover, the Office of the Census does not count the third generation of Puerto Ricans on the continent (children of parents born in the United States). By 1974, the Office of the Census declared that there were significantly more than 1.5 million people born in Puerto Rico or of Puerto Rican parentage, but other reliable sources allege that the Census underestimated the number of Puerto Ricans by 40% or more.

TABLE 10.

POPULATION BY AGE GROUPS OF THE UNITED STATES
AND OF PUERTO RICANS IN THE UNITED STATES, 1974

	Percentage of Total United States Population	Percentage of Total Puerto Ricans in the U.S.A.
Younger than 5 years	7.9	14.5
from 5 to 9	8.5	13.3
from 10 to 17	15.9	18.9
from 18 to 20	5.6	5.3
from 21 to 24	6.8	7.4
from 25 to 34	13.9	17.7
from 35 to 44	10.9	10.1
from 45 to 54	11.4	7.5
from 55 to 64	9.2	3.8
64 and older	9.9	1.6
Average age	28.5 years	19.8 years*

SOURCE: Office of the Census of the United States, Report of the Present Population. "Persons of Spanish Origin in the United States: March 1974". Series P-20, no. 267, July 1974, Table 2, p. 3.

*In 1970, the average age of the 783,000 Puerto Rican migrants in the United States (those born in Puerto Rico) was 30.0 years; however, the average age of the 646,000 Puerto Ricans born in the United States was only 9.3 years, which shows how young the second generation is.

TABLE 11.

CATEGORIES OF EMPLOYMENT OF PUERTO RICANS 16 YEARS OF AGE
AND OLDER IN CONTINENTAL UNITED STATES, 1970

	Number of People
Male Employed	
Professional, technical and kindred workers	12,227
Managers and administrators (except farm)	10,945
Sales workers	10,982
Clerical	27,703
Craftsmen, foremen	41,210
Operators, including transport	87,979
Laborers (except farm)	20,915
Farmers and farm managers	165
Farm laborers and foremen	3,636
Service workers (except private household)	45,799
Private household workers	230
TOTAL	261,791
Female Employed	
Professional, technical and kindred workers	8,870
Managers and administrators (except farm)	1,974
Sales workers	5,399
Clerical	36,349
Craftsmen, foremen	2,990
Operators, including transport	48,738
Laborers (except farm)	1,319
Farmers and farm managers	38
Farm laborers and foremen	384
Service workers (except private household)	15,166
Private household workers	1,190
TOTAL	122,417

SOURCE: *1970 Census of the United States,* "Puerto Ricans in the United States," PC(2)-1E, Table 7.

TABLE 12.

AVERAGE SCHOOL YEARS COMPLETED BY PUERTO RICANS
IN THE UNITED STATES AND IN PUERTO RICO, 1950-1970

| | | IN THE UNITED STATES | | |
	ALL	Born in the U.S.A.	Born in Puerto Rico	IN PUERTO RICO
1950				
Male, 25 years and older	8.2	8.0	9.8	4.1
Female 25 years and older	8.0	7.5	10.1	3.3
1960				
Male, 14 years and older	8.4	8.2	10.3	6.1
Female, 14 years and older	8.2	8.0	10.8	5.6
1970				
Male and female				
25 years and older	8.6	8.4	11.5	6.9

SOURCES: Report of the Census (1950), PE-3D, Table 4, pp. 3 D-13; Report of the Census (1960), PC(SI)-34, Table 42, p. 9; Report of the Census (1960), PC(2)-1D, Table 2, pp.12,14,16; Report of the Census (1970), PC(2)-1E, Table 4, p. 34; Report of the Census (1970), PC(1)-D53 P.R., Table 80, p. 249.

TABLE 13.

PARTICIPATION IN LABOR FORCE OF THE TOTAL U.S. POPULATION
AND OF PERSONS OF SPANISH ORIGIN BY AGE AND SEX, 1972

| | | SPANISH ORIGIN | | |
	TOTAL	Total*	Mexicans	Puerto Ricans
Total number of men	52,900	2,039	1,175	295
from 16 to 24 years	11,938	439	296	60
from 25 to 44 years	23,267	1,108	612	182
from 45 to 64 years	17,695	492	267	53
Total percentage of men	86.0	85.0	86.5	76
from 16 to 24 years	68.2	64.7	70.1	53
from 25 to 44 years	96.1	95.4	96.5	88
from 45 to 64 years	88.2	88.0	88.1	**
Total number of women	31,876	1,055	538	108
from 16 to 24 years	8,377	331	217	28
from 25 to 44 years	12,593	497	241	58
from 45 to 64 years	10,906	227	80	22
Total percentage of women	49.8	40.2	38.8	26
from 16 to 24 years	49.9	42.7	47.1	24
from 25 to 44 years	50.1	40.7	38.3	27
from 45 to 64 years	49.3	36.1	27.0	25

SOURCE: Office of the Census of the United States, Report of the present population, Series P-20, no. 238, July 1973, p. 6.

*Includes other persons of Spanish origin.
**Base less than 75 000

143

TABLE 14.

PERCENTAGE OF PARTICIPATION IN U.S. LABOR FORCE BY WHITE, BLACK
AND PUERTO RICAN MEN BY AGE GROUP, 1970

AGE	NORTH AMERICANS		PUERTO RICANS IN THE U.S.A.		
	White	Black	All	Born in Puerto Rico	Born in the U.S.A.
14-15	14.3	8.8	7.2	8.7	6.3
16-17	37.8	22.5	39.2*	44.3*	33.1*
18-19	61.1	51.6	—	—	—
20-24	81.6	75.6	79.6	81.3	73.2
25-34	94.7	87.5	87.2	87.3	87.0
35-44	95.6	88.4	88.2	87.9	90.1
45-64	88.0	80.0	78.2	77.9	82.1
65 and over	24.9	23.7	20.8	20.7	22.3

NOTE: The figures with asterisks indicate ages from 16 to 19.

SOURCES: *1970 Census of the United States,* "Summary of the United States," PC(1)–C1, Table 78, pp. 1–372; *1970 Census of the United States,* "Puerto Ricans in the United States," PC92–1E, Table 6, pp. 54–55.

TABLE 15.

PERCENTAGE OF PARTICIPATION IN LABOR FORCE BY WOMEN WITH CHILDREN
AND IN CATEGORIES OF WHITE, BLACK AND SPANISH ANCESTRY, 1970

	Total	Children Under 6 Years	Children from 6 to 17 Years	No Child under 18 Years
White	40.6	28.4	49.0	41.5
Black	47.5	47.6	59.8	43.4
Spanish Ancestry	38.1	28.4	43.5	41.5
Mexican	37.8	29.8	43.3	40.1
Puerto Rican	29.9	16.6	30.5	39.9
Cuban	47.1	38.6	59.7	45.1

SOURCE: *Monthly Labor Review,* April 1973, p. 5.

TABLE 16.

Official and Adjusted Employment for the Total Population of the United States
and for Puerto Ricans in the United States, 1972

	United States Total			Puerto Ricans in the United States				
	Size of Labor Force	Percentage in labor force	Percentage of unemployment	Size of labor force	Percentage in labor force	Percentage of unemployment	Adjusted* size of labor force	Adjusted* percentage of unemployment
Men from 16 to 64 years	52,900,000	86.0	6.0	295,000	76.6	8.8	331,000	18.7
Women from 16 to 64 years	31,877,000	49.8	6.6	108,000	26.3	17.6	204,000	56.4
Total	84,777,000	100.0	6.2	403,000	100.0	12.6	535,000	33.0

*The adjusted figures for Puerto Ricans are based on the percentages in the labor force for the entire U.S. population.

SOURCES: *1970 Census of the United States,* "Puerto Ricans in the United States," PC(2)-IE, Table 6, pp. 54–55. *1970 Census of the United States,* "Summary of the United States," PC(1)-C1, Table 78, pp. 1–372.

NOTES

PROLOGUE
1. See *Labor Migration Under Capitalism: the Puerto Rican Experience* (New York: Monthly Review Press, 1979).

INTRODUCTION
1. *Puerto Rico: A Socio-Historic Interpretation.* Translated by Elena Vialo. (New York: Random House, 1972).
2. Pedro Pietri, *Puerto Rican Obituary* (New York: Monthly Review, 1973). See Alfredo Matilla and Iván Silén, *The Puerto Rican Poets* (New York: Bantam Books, 1972).
3. Piri Thomas, *Down These Mean Streets* (New York: Random House, 1967).
4. See his articles in the journal, *The Rican*. Also, the illuminating contribution of the historian Dr. Adalberto López deserves to be emphasized here. See his article, "The Puerto Rican Diaspora," in Adalberto López and James Petras, *Puerto Rico and Puerto Ricans* (New York: Schenk Publishing Company, 1974).
5. Dr. Senior's study was done at the request of the Commission on the Status of the United States and Puerto Rico, and appears as an appendix to his article, "Towards a Balance Sheet of Puerto Rican Migration," in *Status of Puerto Rico; Selected Background Studies Prepared for the United States; Puerto Rico Commission on the Status of Puerto Rico.* (1966). pp. 689-795.
6. This study has been republished in 1970 by Russell and Russell of New York.

CHAPTER 1.
1. Two recently published books offer support for this affirmation: *Modos de producción en América Latina, by* Assadourian, Cardoso and others (Buenos Aires: Cuadernos de Pasado y Presente, 1973) and Cesare Luporini and Emilio Sereni, *El Concepto de Formación Económico-Social* (Buenos Aires: Cuadernos de Pasado y Presente, 1973). Of equal importance are two books by Samir Amin: *Unequal Development: an Essay on the Social Formations of Peripheral Capitalism* (New York: Monthly Review Press, 1976); and his great work, *Accumulation on a World Scale; A Critique of the Theory of Underdevelopment* (New York: Monthly Review Press, 1974).
2. Juan Carlos Garavaglia, "Introducción" to the book *Modos de producción en América Latina, op. cit.*
3. See Manuel Maldonado-Denis, "Hacia una interpretación de historia de Puerto Rico," *Casa de las Américas* (Havana), year XV, no. 86, September-October, 1974.
4. Omar Argüello, "Migración y cambio estructural," in Consejo Nacional de Ciencias Sociales, *Migración y desarrollo-consideraciones teóricas y aspectos socioeconómicos y políticos* (Buenos Aires, 1973), pp. 38-39.
5. For a precise critique of positivism seen from the perspective of critical thought, see Michael Lowy, "Objetividad y punto de vista de clase en las Ciencias Sociales," *Sociedad y Desarrollo* (Santiago de Chile), no. 2, April-June, 1972, pp. 37-54.
6. Octavio Ianni (editor), *Populismo y contradicciones de la clase en Latinoamérica*

(México: Ediciones Era, 1973), p. 85. Also by the same author, *La formación del estado pupulista en América Latina* (México: Ediciones Era, 1975).

7. See Angel Quintero Rivera, "El desarrollo de las clases sociales y los conflictos políticos en Puerto Rico," in Rafael Ramírez et al., Problemas de desigualdad social en Puerto Rico (Río Piedras: Ediciones Librería Internacional, 1972).

8. See my book, *Puerto Rico: a Socio-Historic Interpretation,* op. cit. Also, by the same author, Puerto Rico: Mito y Realidad, second edition (Barcelona: Ediciones Peninsula, 1973).

9. Paul Singer, *Dinámica de la población y desarrollo* (México: Siglo XXI, 1971), p. 26.

10. Ved P. Duggal, *Two papers on the economy of Puerto Rico* (San Germán: The Caribbean Institute and Study Center for Latin America, 1973), p. 8.

11. "Effects of Agricultural and Manufacturing Employment on Internal Migration," in Puerto Rican Planning Board, *Puerto Rican Migrants; A Socio-Economic Study,* (1972).

12. José Luis Vázquez Calzada, "Aspectos demográficos de la Población" (1974), manuscript.

13. Karl Marx, *Capital* (New York: International Publishers, 1967), vol. I, p. 639.

14. *Ibid.,* pp. 631-632.

15. *Ibid.,* p. 641.

16. *Ibid.,* p. 642.

17. *Ibid.,* p. 643.

18. *Ibid.,* pp. 643-644. We consider it important to mention in the present context the interesting polemic between Professor José Nun and Fernando Henrique Cardoso on this subject. See José Nun, "Superpoblación relativa, ejército industrial de reserva y masa marginal," *Revista Latinoamericana de Ciencias* (Santiago de Chile), June-December, 1971. See also Brinley Thomas, *Migration and Economic Growth,* second edition (Cambridge University Press, 1973), p. 7ff.

19. Karl Marx, *A Contribution to the Critique of Political Economy* (New York: International Publishers, 1970), p. 20. The emphasis is the author's.

20. Karl Marx, *The 18th Brumaire of Louis Bonaparte* (New York: International Publishers, 1963), p. 15.

21. Harry Braverman, *Labor and Monopoly Capital* (New York: Monthly Review Press, 1974), pp. 384-385.

22. United Nations Social and Economic Council, *The Welfare Workers and Their Families,* Report of Secretary General. E/CN/515, October 14, 1974.

23. United Nations Economic and Social Council, *Exploitation of Labor Through Illicit and Clandestine Trafficing.* E/CN. 4/Sub. 2/352. 14 August 1974.

24. Angel G. Quintero Rivera, *La clase obrera y el proceso político en Puerto Rico* (Centro de Investigaciones Sociales. U.P.R., 1974). For more about Matienzo Cintrón, see the book by Dr. Louis M. Díaz Soler, *Rosendo Matienzo Cintrón, originador y guardián de una cultura* (Two volumes) Universidad de Puerto Rico: Ediciones del Instituto de Literatura Puertorriqueña, 1960).

25. The complete test of the report appeared in *The San Juan Star* (September 28, 1974).

CHAPTER 2.

1. José Luis Vázquez Calzada, "La emigración puertorriqueña: solución o problema?" *Revista de Ciencias Sociales* (vol. VIII, no. 5, December, 1963).

2. See José Hernández Alvarez, *Return Migration to Puerto Rico* (University of California, 1967). Also, Vázquez Calzada, "Aspectos Demográficos de la Emigración" (manuscript). For the study of the return to Puerto Rico, see also the recent study by Celia Fernández de Cintrón and Pedro Vales Hernández, *Return Migration to Puerto Rico* (Centro de Investigaciones Sociales, University of Puerto Rico, 1974).

3. Informe del Subcomité del grupo de trabajo del Gobernador, Area I *Oportunidades de Empleo, Educación y Adiestramiento,* (Nov. 1973), p. 65 (manuscript).
4. *El Mundo,* April 20, 1974.
5. *Avance,* June 10, 1974, p. 15.
6. *Ibid.,* p. 16.
7. I use the term "antidevelopment" in this context following the felicitous conception of Héctor Malavé Matta when he describes it as that "incessant superficial metamorphosis of prolonged colonization." Héctor Malavé Matta, *Formación histórica del antidesarrollo en Venezuela* (Havana: Casa de las Américas, 1974).
8. Paul Singer, Dinámica de la población y desarrollo (México: Siglo XXI Editores, 1971).
9. This preoccupation, just like the new imperialist strategy to confront the demands of the Third World, can be seen in Secretary of State Kissinger's speech before the U.N. on September 2, 1975. (*The New York Times,* September 2, 1975). See also Jose Consuegra Higgins, *El control de la natalidad como arma del imperialismo* (Buenos Aires: Galerna, 1969).
10. Samir Amin, *El desarrollo desigual* (Barcelona: Ediciones Fontanella, 1974), p. 378.
11. We should now add to the list of apocalyptic prophets professor Juan Sánchez Viera, fiery ideologue of the population catastrophe. But no one overlooks of course the epitome of the "Family Planners," Dr. Silva Inglesias. In some of his recent declarations, the delirious context of which cannot escape the careful reader, he says: "If Puerto Rico's population growth is not controlled to a substitute population rate, population density will reach a crisis of such magnitude as is only contemplated in novels of science fiction. It is well known by behavioral psychologists that when *experimental animal populations* are confined in limited areas, a marked antisocial behavior develops among them, such as cannibalism, low tension resistance, homosexuality and other problems. This experience could well be what we are beginning to see in our society." *El Mundo,* July 22, 1975. Note the analogy between the animal and social world and that the speaker is the Associate Secretary of Health for Family Planning.
12. Barry Commoner, "How Poverty Breeds Overpopulation (and not the other way around)" Ramparts (California), August, September, 1975, p. 23.

CHAPTER 3.

1. See Carmelo Rosario Natal, *Puerto Rico y la crisis de la guerra hispanoamericana* (San Juan: Ramallo Brothers, 1975).
2. José A. Herrero, Víctor Sánchez Cardona and Elías Gutierrez, "La Politica monetaria del '98," in *El Nuevo Día,* July 30, 1975.
3. Charles H. Allen, *Governor of Puerto Rico, First Annual Report Covering the Period from May 1, 1900 to May 1, 1901.* (Government Printing Office, 1901), pp. 74-75.
4. Igualdad Iglesias de Pagán, El obrerismo en Puerto Rico—época de Santiago Iglesias (1896-1905). (Palencia de Castilla: Ediciones Juan Ponce de León, 1973), p. 41.
5. Quoted in Iglesias de Pagán, *Ibid.,* p. 156.
6. The bibliography with respect to Hawaii, but especially concerning Puerto Rican emigrants, has to be taken from sources which only touch our subject indirectly. See, for example, the following books and articles: Romanzo Adams, *Interracial Marriage in Hawaii* (New York: MacMillan, 1937); Francine du Plessis Gray, *Hawaii: The Sugar Coated Fortress* (New York: Random House, 1972); Andrew W. Lind, *An Island Community* (The University of Chicago Press, 1938); Paul Jacobs and Saul Landau, "The Other Side of the Paradise: Hawaii's Forgotten Past," *Social Policy* (New York), Vol. 1, no. 2, July-August, 1970; Sydney Mintz, "Puerto Rican

Emigration: A Three-Fold Comparison," *Social and Economic Studies* (Kingston, Jamaica), vol. 1, no. 4, 1955.
7. José de Diego, *Obras completas,* Two volumes (San Juan: Instituto de Cultura Puertorriqueña, 1966), vol. 1, pp. 24-25.
8. Susan Jacoby, "Immigration Is At Its Highest Point in Half a Century," *The New York Times,* June 8, 1975, p. 7.
9. *La Correspondencia de Puerto Rico,* August 28, 1926. According to what was recorded in a newspaper interview in order to sign the contract with the Puerto Rican authorities a Mr. E. J. Walker would come to Puerto Rico. See *La Democracia,* August 26, 1924.
10. *La Democracia,* September 9, 1926.
11. *Ibid.* (The emphasis is the author's.)
12. Carey MacWilliams, *111 Fares the Land* (Boston: Little, Brown, 1942), pp. 79-80. We have not been able to prove whether there was a riot or whether the total that appeared at the Port of San Juan was 6,000 people. What we do know is that there was a great crowding and that the bitterness of those who came was expressed vociferously.
13. *La Democracia,* September 10, 1926.
14. *La Correspondencia de Puerto Rico,* Ocotober 23, 1926.
15. Clarence Senior, *The Puerto Rican Migrant in Saint Croix* (University of Puerto Rico: Social Science Research Center, 1947).
16. Gordon K. Lewis, *The Virgin Islands* (Northwestern University Press, 1972), p. 207.
17. See the article by Mintz to which we alluded in note 6 of this chapter.
18. Lawrence R. Chenault, The Puerto Rican Migrant in New York City (New York: Russell and Russell, 1970), p. 55.

CHAPTER 4.

1. *The San Juan Star,* August 7, 1974. According to the most recent computation, the total Puerto Rican population residing in New York City is 811,143, a figure strongly disputed by Puerto Rican leaders in New York. *New York Times,* October 2, 1972.
2. See the "Declaración de la seccional de Estados Unidos del Partido Socialista Puertorriqueño," which appeared in a special issue of the journal *Nueva Lucha;* also see the Report of the United States Commission on Civil Rights, *Counting the Forgotten: The 1970 Census Count of Persons of Spanish Speaking Background in the United States,* April 1974. A recent study of the Bureau of Applied Research of Columbia University contributes some interesting statistics on this subject. See A. J. Jaffe and Zaida Carreras Carleton, *Some Demographic and Economic Characteristics of the Puerto Rican Population Living on the Mainland U.S.A.* (Columbia University: Bureau of Applied Research, November, 1974).
3. See the interesting article by Professor Raymond M. Otero Aurinaga, where he estimates that there are some 100,000 Puerto Ricans living in the state of California. "The Califorricans," *The San Juan Star Magazine,* April, 1974.
4. According to the latest census, the distribution of the Puerto Rican population by boroughs in New York City in 1970 was the following: Bronx (316,772 or 21.5% of the total); Brooklyn (271,769 or 10.4%); Manhattan (185,323 or 12%); Queens (33,141 or 1.7%) and Staten Island (4,838 or 1.6%). The figures are from the 1972 census and they indicate a total Puerto Rican population of 811,843 (10% of the city's population). (*The New York Times,* October 2, 1972). The figure, as we have said, is considerably greater, but the proportionate distribution by borough is accurate.
5. *El Mundo,* September 8, 1975.
6. Edward C. Burks, "Affluence Eludes Blacks, Puerto Ricans," *The New York Times,*

August 18, 1972. An even more recent report by Kal Wagenheim confirms this tendency. See *The New York Times*, June 10, 1975.

7. *The New York Times*, October 25, 1971.
8. *The New York Times*, March 26, 1970.
9. Nathan Glazer and Daniel Patrick Moynihan, *Beyond the Melting Pot*, second edition (Cambridge: MIT Press, 1970), p. 20.
10. Richard Goldstein, "The Big Mango," *New York Magazine*, August 7, 1972, p. 24.
11. Lawrence R. Chenault, *The Puerto Rican Migrant in New York City* (New York: Russell and Russell, 1970), pp. 157-158. This book was published for the first time in 1938.
12. C. Wright Mills, et al., *The Puerto Rican Journey* (New York: Russell and Russell, 1967), pp. 73, 82. This book was originally published by Harper and Row in 1950. Its findings, however, cover essentially the period up to 1948.
13. Eva E. Sandis, "Characteristics of Puerto Rican Migrants to and from the United States," in Francesco Cordasco and Eugene Buccioni (editors), *The Puerto Rican Experience* (New Jersey: Littlefield Adams, 1975), p. 138.
14. Kal Wagenheim, *A Survey of Puerto Ricans in the U.S. Mainland in the 1970's* (New York: Praeger, 1975), p. 41.
15. *Ibid.*, p. 22. Actually, the so-called poverty line overlooks things that refer to the maldistribution of self-respect, educational opportunities, social mobility and participation in various forms of decision-making. See Bertram Gross in his review of Fox and Piven, *Regulating the Poor*, cited before, in Social Policy (New York), May-June, 1972, p. 58.
16. *Ibid.*, pp. 27-28. Professor Bertram Gross has arrived at the conclusion that there are 25.6 million people unemployed in the United States, that is to say, 24.6% of the work force, if we truly take into consideration underemployment, non-apparent unemployment, the number of people who are no longer in the work force because they have tired from looking for work and not finding any. See Bertram Gross and Stanley Moses, "Measuring the Real Work Force: 25 million unemployed," in Social Policy, September-October, 1972.
17. *New York Times*, September 21, 1972. Quoted in Wagenheim, *op. cit.*, p. 68.
18. *New York Times*, January 30, 1975.

CHAPTER 5.
1. Ricardo Puerta, "El puertorriqueño invisible," in *La Escalera* (Rio Piedras), vol. VI, no. 2, May, 1972, p. 22.
2. *Informe de la Comisión Especial para investigar los campamentos y fincas agrícolas en diferentes sitios de los Estados Unidos.* (Report of the Special Commission to Investigate the Agricultural Camps and Farms in Different Places of the United States.) Seventh Legislative Assembly, Third Ordinary Session, April, 1975. The Special Commission was presided over by Representative Teófilo Morales. See also the articles by the reporter Darío Carlo in *El Mundo*, September 29, and 30, 1974.
3. Thomas Hibben and Rafael Pico, *Industrial Development of Puerto Rico and the Virgin Isles of the United States*, Report of the United States Caribbean Commission, 1948, p. 107. I owe the finding of this reference to my reading it in a recently published book by Luis Nieves Falcón. See Luis Nieves Falcón, *El emigrante puertorriqueño* (Río Piedras: Edil, 1975), p. 4.
4. Junta de Planifacación de Puerto Rico (Planning Board of Puerto Rico), negociado de Estadísticas del Trabajo, *Informe* economico al gobernador, 1955, p. 99. The report was submitted by Mr. Oliveras on August 1, 1955. Taken from Dr. Nieves Falcón's recently cited book.
5. The figures and information are taken from an article signed by José A. Castrodad

under the title "Fomentan Emigración Braceros E. U." in *El Imparcial* (San Juan, Puerto Rico), May 17, 1972.
6. Ricardo Puerta, "El puertorriqueño invisible," *op. cit.,* p. 29.
7. *Claridad,* August 18, 1975. See also the newspapers *El Mundo, El Nuevo Día* and *The San Juan Star* of the same date.
8. Gary S. Goodpastor, Associate Professor of Law, University of Iowa, *Public Regulation of Working Conditions in Agriculture* prepared for the use of the House Committee on Education and Labor Subcommittee on Agriculture Labor, United States House of Representatives, May 21, 1971, pp. 48-49. (manuscript)

CHAPTER 6.

1. Manuel Maldonado-Denis, *Puerto Rico: Mito y Realidad.*
2. See, with respect to this: Aida Negrón de Montilla, *Americanization in Puerto Rico and the Public School System 1900-1930* (Río Piedras, Edil, 1971); Germán de Granda, *Transculturación e interferencia lingüística en el Puerto Rico contemporáneo (1898-1968)* (Bogota: Instituto Caro y Cuervo, 1968); Silvia Viera, "El Bilingüismo de los puertorriqueños: un mito politico=docente," in *Carvelle,* no. 18, 1972; and Elizier Narváez, "Anglicismo y Spanglish: Dos males y una sola causa," in *Penelope y El Mundo Nuevo,* June-August, 1973.
3. Nathan Glazer and Daniel Moynihan, *Beyond the Melting Pot,* second edition (Cambridge: M.I.T. Press, 1971).
4. See in this respect the interesting book by Colin Greer (ed.), *Divided Society* (New York: Basic Books, 1974) and Milton Gordon, *Assimilation in American Life, The Role of Race, Religion and National* Origins (Oxford University Press, 1964).
5. Eduardo Seda Bonilla, *Requiem para una Cultura* (Río Piedras: Ediciones Bayoán, 1974), p. 223.
6. In a recent book, Professor Isabelo Zenón Cruz has made a series of interesting points about the problem of racism in Puerto Rico. The book suffers nevertheless from serious methodological errors in spits of its usefulness. See his *Narciso descubre su trasero* (Humacao, 1975). Dr. Seda Bonilla, in his *Requiem para una cultura,* op. cit., has treated the subject with greater precision in pointing out the distinction between race and color as the crux of the racial question, showing how this affects *Boricuas* in the United States.
7. Milton M. Gordon, *Assimilation in American Life* (Oxford University Press, 1964), pp. 72-73, 129.
8. See with respect to this, Carlos Varo, *Consideraciones antropológicas y políticas en torno a la esencia del "Spanglish" en Nueva York* (Río Piedras: Ediciones Librería Internacional, 1971).
9. See *The New York Times,* May 5, 1972, August 7, 1972 and March 12, 1975. In addition, consult the important study by the Board of Education of New York City entitled *The Puerto Rican Study 1953-1957* (New York City: Board of Education, 1958).
10. Seda Bonilla, *op. cit.,* pp. 276-277.
11. Karl Marx, *The German Ideology* (New York: International Publishers, 1970), pp. 64-65.
12. Luis Rafael Sánchez, "La Generación del O Sea," in *Claridad* (San Juan), January 23, 1972, p. 22.
13. Armand Mattelart, Petricio Biedman, and Santiago Funes, *Comunicación masiva y revolución socialista* (Santiago: Editorial Prensa Latinoamericana, 1971), p. 23. See also with regard to this, number 77 of *Casa de las Américas* (Havana), dedicated to the subject of "Imperialism and Mass Means of Communication," also, Ariel Dorfman and Armand Mattelart, *Para Leer al Pato Donald* (Valparaiso: Ediciones Universitarias de Valparaiso, 1971).

14. This is taken from a list from the American Association of State Colleges and Universities. Quoted in John Chapman, "Hypometropia; A Long Overdue Critique of Latin American Studies," *Journal of Contemporary Puerto Rican Thought,* vol. II, nos. 2 and 3, p. 22.

15. Frank Bonilla and Emilio González, "New Knowing, New Practices: Puerto Rican Studies," in Frank Bonilla and Robert Girling (eds.), *Structures of Dependency* (New York, 1973), p. 231.

16. Eduardo Seda Bonilla, *Requiem para una cultura* (Rio Piedras: Ediciones Bayoan, 1974), p. 285.

17. See the special issue of *Journal of Contemporary Puerto Rican Thought,* vol. I, No. 4, dedicated to this subject.

CHAPTER 7.

1. This ideological tendency is uniquely expressed in the work of writers such as René Marqués and Abelardo Díaz Alfaro, among others. I refer the interested reader to my essay, "La temática social en la literatura puertorriqueña," in *Puerto Rico: Mito y Realidad,* second edition (Barcelona: Peninsula, 1972).

2. José Hernández Alvarez, *Return Migration to Puerto Rico* (Berkeley: University of California, 1967), p. 104.

3. *Ibid.,* p. 104.

4. Paul Baran and Paul Sweezy, *Monopoly Capital* (New York: *Monthly Review Press,* 1966), p. 267.

5. Harry Braverman, "Work and Unemployment," *Monthly Review* (New York), June, 1975, p. 30.

6. Kal Wagenheim, *A Survey of Puerto Ricans on the U.S. Mainland in the 1970s* (New York: Praeger, 1975), pp. 68-70.

7. Quoted in E. Seda Bonilla, *Requiem para una cultura* (Rio Piedras: Edil, 1974), pp. 276-277.

8. Samir Amin, *Accumulation on a World Scale, op. cit.,* vol. 1, pp. 26-27.

9. See the interesting, although sometimes unbalanced, article by Dr. Eduardo Seda Bonilla, "Qué somos: puertorriqueños, neorriqueños o niuyorriqueños?" *Journal of Contemporary Puerto Rican Thought; The Rican* (Wisconsin), vol. 11, nos. 2-3, pp. 81-107.

10. I refer the interested reader to my essay "Franz Fanon y el pensamiento anti-colonialista contemporáneo" in my book *Puerto Rico: mito y realidad* (Barcelona: Ediciones Peninsula, 1972).

FINAL OBSERVATIONS

1. The first draft of the Tobin Report was submitted on August 1, 1975. The "Committee to Study the Finances of Puerto Rico," besides including Dr. Tobin, also included Drs. Bernard Wasow (New York University) and Richard Porter (University of Michigan).

BIBLIOGRAPHY

Amin, Samir. *Accumulation on a World Scale* (New York: Monthly Review Press, 1974.)
—— *Unequal Development* (New York: Monthly Review Press, 1976.)
—— *Capitalismo periférico y comercio internacional* (Buenos Aires: Ediciones Periferia, 1974.)
Babín, María Teresa and Steiner, Stan (editors). *Borinquen: an Anthology of Puerto Rican Literature* (New York: Random House, 1974.)
Bambirra, Vania. *El capitalismo dependiente latinoamericano* (México: Fondo de Cultura Económica, 1959.)
Baran, Paul. *The Political Economy of Growth* (New York: Monthly Review Press, 1969.)
—— and Sweezy, Paul. *Monopoly Capital* (New York: Monthly Review Press, 1966.)
Beckford, George L. *Persistent Poverty-Underdevelopment in Plantation Economies of the Third World* (New York: Oxford University Press, 1972.)
Berle, Beatrice B. *80 Puerto Rican Families in New York City* (Columbia University Press, 1958.)
Bonilla, Frank and Girling, Robert (editors). *Structures of Dependency* (New York, 1973.)
Braverman, Harry. *Labor and Monopoly Capital* (New York: Monthly Review Press, 1974.)
Burma, John H. *Spanish-Speaking Groups in the United States* (Duke University Press, 1954.)
Caplovitz, David, et. al. *The Poor Pay More* (Free Press, 1963.)
Cardoso, F. M. and Falleto, Enzo. *Dependencia y desarrollo en América Latina* (México: Siglo XXI, 1969.)
Cardoso, Fernando H. "Comentario sobre los conceptos de sobrepoblación relativa y marginalidad," *Revista Latinoamericana de Ciencias Sociales* (Santiago de Chile, June-December, 1971.)
Center for Migration Studies, Staten Island, New York. "The Puerto Rican Experience on the United States Mainland," *International Migration Review* (New York), vol. II, Spring, 1968.
Cifre de Loubreiel, Estela. *La inmigración a Puerto Rico durante el siglo xix* (San Juan: Instituto de Cultura Puertorriqueña, 1964.)
Cintrón, Celia and Vales, Pedro. *A Pilot Study: Return Migration to Puerto Rico* (Centro de Investigaciones Sociales de la Universidad de Puerto Rico, 1974.)
Consejo Latinoamericano de Ciencias Sociales (CLASCO). *Migración y desarrollo— consideraciones teóricas y aspectos socio-económicos y políticos* (Buenos Aires, 1973.)
Consuegra, José. *El control de la natalidad como arma del imperialismo* (Buenos Aires: Galerna, 1973.)
Cordasco, Francisco and Buccioni, Eugene (editors). *The Puerto Rican Experience* (New Jersey: Littlefield Adams, 1973.)
Chenault, Lawrence. *The Puerto Rican Migrant in New York City* (Columbia University Press, 1938.)

De Diego, José. *Obras completas,* two volumes (San Juan: Instituto de Cultura Puerto-
rriqueña, 1966.)
De Granda, Germán. *Transculturación e interferencia lingüïstica en el Puerto Rico
contemporáneo (1898-1968)* (Bogotá: Instituto Caro y Cuervo, 1968.)
Duggal, Ved. P. *Two Papers on the Economy of Puerto Rico* (San German, Inter-
american University of Puerto Rico, 1973.)
Dworkis, Martin. *Impact of Puerto Rican Migration on Governmental Services in New
York City* (New York University Press, 1957.)
Fernández, Méndez, Eugenio (editor). *Portrait of a Society; Readings on Puerto Rican
Sociology* (Universidad de Puerto Rico, 1972.)
Fitzpatrick, Joseph P. *The Puerto Rican Americans* (New York: Prentice Hall, 1971.)
———— (Fr.) "Intermarriage of Puerto Ricans in New York City," *The American Journal
of Sociology,* vol. LXXI, no. 4, January 1966, pp. 395-406.
Frank, Andre Gunder. *Capitalism and Underdevelopment in Latin America* (New York:
Monthly Review Press, 1969.)
———— Cockroft, J. D. and Johnson, Dale N. *Economía política del subdesarrollo en
América Latina* (Buenos Aires: Ediciones Signos, 1970.)
Fucaraccio, A. et. al. *Imperialismo y control de la población* (Buenos Aires: Ediciones
Periferia, 1973.)
Lewis, Oscar. *La Vida; A Puerto Rican Family in the Culture of Poverty: San Juan and
New York* (New York: Random House, 1966.)
López, Adalberto and Petras, James (editors). *Puerto Rico and Puerto Ricans; Studies in
History and Society* (New York: Schenk Publishing Company, 1974.)
López, Alfredo. *The Puerto Rican Papers* (New York: Bobbs Merrill, 1973.)
Luporini, Cesare and Serini, Emilio (editors). *El concepto de "formación económico-
social"* (Buenos Aires: Cuadernos de Pasado y Presente, 1973.)
Malavé, Mata, Héctor. *Formación histórica del antidesarrollo en Venezuela* (Havana:
Casa de las Américas, 1975.)
Maldonado-Denis, Manuel. *Puerto Rico: mito y realidad* (Barcelona: Ediciones Penin-
sula, 1973.)
———— *Puerto Rico: A Socio-Historic Interpretation* (New York: Random House, 1972.)
Marini, Ruy Mauro. *Dialéctica de la dependencia* (México: Ediciones Era, 1973.)
Marx, Karl. *Capital* three volumes (New York: International Publishers, 1967.)
———— *A Contribution to the Critique of Political Economy* (New York: International
Publishers, 1970.)
Mathews, Thomas G. *Puerto Rican Politics and the New Deal* (Gainesville: University of
Florida Press, 1960.)
Matilla, Alfredo and Silen, Iván (editors). *The Puerto Rican Poets* (New York: Bantam
Books, 1972.)
Morrison, J. Cayce. *The Puerto Rican Study: 1953-1957* (New York City Board of
Education, 1958.)
Negrón de Montilla, Aida. *Americanization in Puerto Rico and the Public School
System 1900-1930* (Río Piedras: Edil, 1971.)
Nieves Falcón, Luis. *Diagnóstico de Puerto Rico* (Río Piedras: Editorial Edil, 1972.)
———— *Los emigrantes puertorriqueños* (Río Piedras: Editorial Edil, 1975.)
Novak, Ernest. *The Rise of the Unmeltable Ethnics* (New York: MacMillan, 1971.)
Nun, José. "Superpoblación relativa, ejército industrial de reserva y masa marginal,"
Revista Latinoamericana de Sociología (Buenos Aires) vol. V, July 1969, no. 2.
Padilla, Elena. *Up from Puerto Rico* (Columbia University Press, 1958.)
———— *Up from Puerto Rico* (Río Piedras: Editorial Juan XXIII, 1974.)
Pietri, Pedro. *Puerto Rican Obituary* (New York: Monthly Review Press, 1974.)
Puerta, Ricardo, "El puertorriqueño invisible," *La Escalera* (Río Piedras, vol. VI, no. 2
May 1972.)

Quijano, Aníbal and Weffort, Francisco. *Populismo, marginalización y dependencia* (Costa Rica: Editorial Universitaria Centroamericana, 1973.)

Quintero Rivera, Angel (editor). *La lucha obrera en Puerto Rico* (Río Piedras: CEREP, 1973.)

——— *La clase obrera y el proceso político en Puerto Rico* (Río Piedras: Centro de Investigaciones Sociales de la Universidad de Puerto Rico, 1972.)

Ramírez, Rafael L. et. al. (editors). *Problemas de desigualdad social en Puerto Rico* (Río Piedras: Ediciones Librería Internacional, 1973.)

Rand, Christopher. *The Puerto Ricans* (Oxford University Press, 1958.)

Reynolds, Lloyd G. and Gregory, Peter. *Wages, Productivity, and Industrialization in Puerto Rico* (Hollywood, Ill: Richard D. Irvin Inc., 1965.)

Riestra, Miguel J. *Colonialismo y pobreza* (San Juan: Ediciones Praxis, 1974.)

Rogler, Lloyd. *Migrant in the City* (New York: Basic Books, 1972.)

Rosario Natal, Carmelo. *Puerto Rico y la crisis de la guerra hispanoamericana* (Hato Rey: Ramallo Brothers, 1975.)

Rose, Arnold M. and Rose, Carolina B. (editors). *Minority Problems* (New York: Harper and Row, 1972.)

Sanchez Albornoz Nicolás. *La población de América Latina* (Madrid: Alianza Editorial, 1973.)

Santiago Meléndez, Jaime. "Puerto Rico—presente y futuro económico—hacia una nueva estrategia," *Boletín de Gerencia Administrativa* (San Juan), March-April, 1975.

Saveth, Edward N. *American Historians and European Immigrants 1875-1925* (Columbia University Press, 1948.)

Seda Bonilla, Eduardo. *Requiem para una cultura* (Río Piedras: Ediciones Bayoán, 1973.)

Segal, Bernard E. (editor) *Racial and Ethnic Relations; Selected Readings* (New York: Crowell, 1966.)

Senior, Clarence. *Our Citizens from the Caribbean* (McGraw-Hill; 1965.)

——— *The Puerto Ricans: Strangers Then Neighbors* (Quadrangle Science Research Center, 1947.)

——— *The Puerto Ricans: Strangers Then Neighbors* (Quadrangle Books, 1965,)

Sexton, Patricia. *Spanish Harlem: Anatomy of Poverty* (Harper and Row, 1965.)

Silén, Juan Angel. *De la guerrilla cívica a la nación dividida* (Río Piedras: Ediciones Puerto, 1975.)

——— *Historia de la nación puertorriqueña* (Río Piedras: Editorial Edil, 1973.)

Singer, Paul. *Dinámica de la población y desarrollo* (México: Siglo XXI, 1971.)

Sweezy, Paul M. *The Theory of Capitalist Development* (New York: Monthly Review Press, 1942.)

Thieme, Frederick P. *The Puerto Rican Population: A Study in Human Biology* (University of Michigan Museum of Anthropology, 1959.)

Thomas, Brinley. *Migration and Economic Growth* (Cambridge University Press, 1973.)

Thomas, Piri. *Down These Mean Streets* (New York: Knopf, 1967.)

Torres, Benjamín (editor). *Pedro Albizu Campos; Obras escogidas,* vol. I (San Juan: Editorial Jelofe, 1975.)

United Nations Social and Economic Council. *Exploitation of Labour Through Illicit and Clandestine Trafficking.* E/cn. 4/sub. 2/352, 14 August 1974.

——— *The Welfare of Migrant Workers and Their Families, Report of the Secretary General.* E/cn. 5/515, 14 October, 1974.

United States-Puerto Rico Commission on the Status of Puerto Rico. *Status of Puerto Rico; Selected Background Studies* (Washington Government Printing Office, 1966.)

Varo, Carlos. *Consideraciones antropológicas y políticas en torno a la enseñanza del "Spanglish" en Nueva York* (Río Piedras: Ediciones Librería Internacional, 1971.)
———— *Puerto Rico: Radiografía de un pueblo asediado* (Río Piedras: Ediciones Puerto Rico, 1973.)
Vázquez Calzada, Jose Luis. "La emigración puertorriqueña: ¿solución o problema? *Revista de Ciencias Sociales de la Universidad de Puerto Rico* (vol. XVII, no. 3, September, 1963.)
———— "La esterilización femenina en Puerto Rico," *Revista de Ciencias Sociales de la Universidad de Puerto Rico* (vol. XVII, no. 3, September, 1973.)
Vilas, Carlos M. et. al. *Imperialismo y clases sociales en el Caribe* (Buenos Aires: Cuenca Ediciones, 1973.)
Wagenheim, Kal. *A Survey of Puerto Ricans on the U.S. Mainland in the 1970's* (New York: Praeger, 1975.)
———— and Wagenheim, Olga Jimenez de (editors). *The Puerto Ricans; A Documentary History* (New York: Praeger, 1973.)
Wakefield, Dan. *Island in the City: Puerto Ricans in New York* (Houghton Mifflin Co., 1959.)
Wells, Henry. *The Modernization of Puerto Rico* (Harvard University Press, 1969.)
Zenón Cruz, Isabelo. *Narciso descubre su trasero,* two volumes (Humacao: Editorial Furidi, 1974-1975.)